Developing Composition Skills

Second Edition

Mary K. Ruetten

THOMSON

HEINLE ™

Australia   Canada   Mexico   Singapore   Spain   United Kingdom   United States

THOMSON

HEINLE

Developing Composition Skills, Second Edition
Rhetoric and Grammar
Mary K. Ruetten

Acquisitions Editor:
Sherrise Roehr

Managing Editor:
James W. Brown

**Associate Developmental
Editor:** *Sarah Barnicle*

Production Editor:
Eunice Yeates-Fogle

Senior Manufacturing Coordinator: *Mary Beth Hennebury*

Contributing Editor:
John Chapman

Editorial Assistant:
Elizabeth Allen

Senior Marketing Manager:
Charlotte Sturdy

**Director, Global ESL Training
and Development:**
Evelyn Nelson

Photo Research:
Sheri Blaney

Cover Design:
Lianne Ames

Composition:
Modern Graphics Inc.

Project Management:
Colophon

Printer:
Quebecor World

Library of Congress Control Number:
2001051967
ISBN 0-8384-2655-7

 This book is printed on acid-free recycled paper.

**Photo and text credits appear on pages 281 and 282 which constitute
a continuation of this copyright page.**

Dedication

To All Current and Returned Peace Corps Volunteers

Acknowledgments

To the many people whose help has been essential in bringing this book to fruition, my heartfelt thanks: to my students, past and present, who have shared their writing and lives with me; to my colleague, Barbara Gaffney, who graciously undertook the task of choosing video clips and writing the video section; to all of the fine people at Heinle, who have carefully guided the book from manuscript to production; and finally, to my husband, Cooper Mackin, who has supported, encouraged, and helped me more than I can ever say.

Mary K. Ruetten

Contents

In this article, high-school teens discuss various sources of stress in their lives and its effects on them.

Chapter 5:   Analyzing Processes   97

This video describes a helpful computer system called ISIS (Integrated Student Information Service), which is used by students at the University of Florida.

This essay was written by Hsin-Chuan Chen when he was a student in an ESL class. It is about an online library catalog system when he was a student in an ESL class.

This article about the different types of taste buds in your mouth was written by Eric Haseltine and published in the magazine *Discover* in February 2000.

To the Teacher

Developing Composition Skills is an intermediate-level writing text for academically bound ESL and EFL students. The program provides paragraph-level writing development, introduction to and use of rhetorical strategies, grammar support, and a rich selection of readings that serve as springboards for writing.

UNDERLYING ASSUMPTIONS

Developing Composition Skills is based on the following assumptions:

1. Reading, writing, and thinking are interrelated activities.
2. To write well, writers must engage with ideas. They must find ideas interesting and connect them to their knowledge and experience. The more that student writers are intrigued by ideas, the more time and effort they will spend in writing about them.
3. Writers must be aware of the context in which they are writing. They must understand the expectations of academic audiences and the ways of thinking that typically fulfill those expectations. Since rhetorical strategies vary from culture to culture, ESL students may not be familiar with the conventions of academic discourse in English. ESL students, therefore, can profit from explicit discussion and analysis of the methods of development and strategies that English-language writers use in academic discourse.
4. Fluency in writing is not to be confused with grammatical accuracy; writers need to develop both. When creating a text, writers focus on rhetorical and organizational issues. Once the text has been drafted, they need to pay attention to grammatical accuracy.

DESIGN OF THE TEXT

Developing Composition Skills addresses these underlying assumptions in the following ways:

1. To engage students' interest, each chapter is organized around a theme. The themes are broad enough so that all students can relate to them; at the same time, they are current, serious, and relevant to an academic setting. Student writers explore the particular theme through journal writing, reading, and discussion. These activities pique students' interest, foster critical thinking, and provide a context for writing assignments.

2. The students' own topics develop from the general theme of the chapter, which is focused enough to allow for unified class discussion but broad enough to generate individualized topics. Interaction with the theme allows students to build a knowledge base and to write about it with complexity.

3. Each chapter focuses on a method of development typically used in academic writing: narration, description, or analysis. Because narration and description are less common in academic writing than analysis, the book focuses mainly on types of analysis: process, comparing/contrasting, classifying, and cause/effect.

4. Each chapter contains samples of both professional and student writing. The professionally written selections serve both to engage students' interest and to exemplify a method of development. Since few writers rely on only one method of development to make their point, the passages reflect a blend of methods. Nevertheless, the primary mode of development is evident in each. The student writings function as examples of a method of development as well. By looking at the choices other writers make, ESL writers can develop awareness of context and method. They learn what is appropriate in academic writing and what rhetorical strategies are available to them. This awareness is crucial for student writers to see their work as part of the academic community.

5. Each chapter offers a variety of activities designed to familiarize students with the concepts of focusing on a main idea, developing support, and organizing a text.

6. Each chapter introduces cohesion devices relevant to the method of development and suggests particular grammar points for futher study. The grammar points are explained and practiced in the Grammar Review in Appendix C. This section, while not intended to cover all of English grammar, is designed to help students use the most common sentence structures and major verb tenses.

ORGANIZATION OF THE TEXT

Developing Composition Skills is organized into eight chapters. The first chapter familiarizes students with the basics of the paragraph form: topic, topic sentence, support, unity, and coherence. This chapter also introduces the writing process, some prewriting techniques, and the uses of the journal. Chapters Two through Eight focus on a specific theme and method of development. Chapter Eight also introduces the essay form.

These chapters contain the following activities:

1. **Getting Started.** Chapters Two through Eight begin with journal writing, inviting students to connect personally to the theme of the chapter and to share their experiences with others. An optional video activity provides another interesting way for students to explore the theme.

2. **Reading.** This section is introduced with photographs or drawings accompanied by discussion questions and is followed by comprehension and discussion questions. New vocabulary is glossed in the left-hand margin. The activities in both the Getting Started and Reading sections are designed to engage students with the theme by activating their background knowledge and by tying their knowledge and experience to the knowledge and experience of others.

3. **Preparing to Write.** This section introduces the main rhetorical points of the chapter and focuses on developing a main point, support, and organization. In this section, students work through the relevant steps in the writing process and, in some chapters, write a paragraph as the last activity.

4. **Writing Assignment.** This section asks students to write a paragraph or essay, starting from the beginning of the writing process. Students prepare to write, then write and revise; revising allows for peer or self evaluation. Students apply rhetorical strategies from the previous section, internalizing the steps of the writing process.

5. **Using Language Effectively.** This section focuses on cohesion and grammar. Students are encouraged to work on accuracy in their writing. An optional Internet activity extends students' knowledge of the chapter's theme and reinforces the rhetorical strategy in speaking and writing.

6. **More Reading and Writing.** This section contains another reading and more topics for writing and discussion. The reading, somewhat more challenging than the earlier one, relates to the chapter's theme and is followed by comprehension and discussion questions. It can be used at the beginning of the chapter in conjunction with the first reading to provide more background and discussion of the topic, or it can be used as a follow-up activity. The topics for writing and discussion are good assignments for journal writing and group activities.

The text includes four appendixes:

    A. A map of the world to use with the readings
    B. Prewriting strategies
    C. The grammar review section
    D. A list of irregular verb forms

The difficult words glossed alongside the readings are gathered into a glossary for easy reference. An index is also included.

FLEXIBILITY OF THE TEXT

Developing Composition Skills is flexible. Throughout the text, the chapters focus on the paragraph; however, the materials in the chapters are easily adaptable to essay writing. Chapter Eight is a complete introduction to the essay, with readings and sample essays. This chapter can be inserted into the course of study at any time, allowing student writing to focus thereafter on multi-paragraph essays.

MAJOR CHANGES IN THE SECOND EDITION

Two major additions in this edition are the CNN Video Activity and the Using the Internet activity. The video activity is designed to engage students in the theme of the chapter and to deepen their understanding of it. The high-interest Internet activity allows students to use the chapter's rhetorical strategy and to see it in use. Other changes in this edition include clearly articulated writing, reading, and grammar goals at the beginning of each chapter, additional grammar activities, and a number of new readings, both student and professional.

ARTICULATION WITH *REFINING COMPOSITION SKILLS*

Developing Composition Skills is an intermediate-level companion to *Refining Composition Skills*. *Developing Composition Skills,* focusing mostly on paragraph writing, introduces students to the conventions of academic writing. *Refining Composition Skills,* beginning with a review of the paragraph, guides students to write with greater depth and complexity on academic topics in the context of the essay.

QUESTIONS AND COMMENTS

If you have questions about any part of the text, or after using it, have comments or feedback, I would appreciate hearing from you via Heinle.

Mary K. Ruetten

Chapter 1 Introducing the Paragraph

Theme

Reasons for Writing

Goals

Writing

To write a paragraph

To understand the parts of a paragraph

To understand the characteristics of a paragraph

To understand and do the writing process

To begin a writing journal

Reading

To read about and reflect on learning to write

Grammar

To review independent and dependent clauses and their punctuation

Getting Started

CNN® Video Activity: Writing off Stress

 People write about their personal experiences and feelings in journals or diaries for many reasons. This video shows therapists and patients who believe writing can reduce stress and help heal some diseases.

Before you watch the video, discuss these questions and review these terms with your classmates or teacher.

1. Do you think writing can help to heal people?
2. How can writing help to heal people?
3. What kinds of illnesses can writing help to heal?
4. Review these terms: chronic   catharsis

Understanding the Video

Comprehension. Read the following questions. As you watch the video, take brief notes. After you watch the video, answer the questions.

1. What are two diseases that writing can help to heal?
2. What sometimes happens to people who keep their feelings inside?
3. What group of people may find writing disturbing?
4. Do the healing effects of writing last for a long time?

Discussion. After you watch the video, discuss these questions with your classmates or teacher.

1. Do you believe diseases are caused by a person's mental health?
2. Do you agree that writing helps to relieve stress or worry? Does it ever cause stress?
3. What are some other reasons for writing in a diary or journal besides its healing effects?
4. Both the doctor and the woman who survived breast cancer emphasize that the mind and body are one. Should doctors and other health workers pay more attention to the whole person, not just the body? If so, in what ways? If not, why not?

Reading

Discuss these questions with your classmates or teacher.

1. Look at the photographs on pages 3 and four. What do you think is the relationship between the people in the first two pictures? In the second two pictures?

2. Tell what you think is happening in each picture.
3. Have you written a letter recently? Who did you write to? What did you write about?

Reading

From Reaching Across the Gap: How I Write
by Michael C. Flanigan

This reading is part of an essay by Michael C. Flanigan, who is a Professor of Composition at the University of Oklahoma. It was published in 1988 in a book entitled *Writers on Writing.*

My sister Mary and my brother Leo were the first two audiences I wrote for. Mary and the boys (four of us) were separated when my father joined the navy at the beginning of World War II. Mary stayed with my mother while we went to St. Francis's Home for Boys to get **discipline**,° uniforms, and cleanly ways. I was five, the youngest in the five-hundred-boy school. I remember how much I wanted to write my sister, so after our daily lessons of reading and **penmanship**° (the rest of school is forgotten) I would return to the dorm in the evening and practice. I wrote and wrote and wrote. All the **initial**° writing was practice—to get my penmanship right, to string words together for sense, to punctuate, to fill a page, then another and another until a pad was gone.

Finally I wrote a letter to my sister. I filled a page with How are you? Hope you are fine. Miss you. Love you. Leo, Pat, and Pete are fine. Leo is growing trees from sticks. Please write. I was not **confident of**° my first attempt at written communication, so I stuffed the letter with jokes from magazines, some buttons I had collected, and a holy medal. All things I knew my sister liked.

Within a week my letter was answered. Besides a thank you for the gifts were descriptions of Mary's new school, how she was learning to ride a bike, and **hosts of**° other information about herself and our mother—three full pages. She asked one question: How does Leo grow trees from sticks? I didn't know. He just told me. I knew I had to find out. When I asked, Leo explained in **minute**° detail how he picked the right branches from trees, cut them, soaked them, and on through a whole fascinating process that I repeated as best I could in my next letter. I also followed my sister's example and told about bits and pieces from our lives at the "military school." Our correspondence continued for over four years until we boys were sent to see my father in Spokane in 1946. The letters stopped on both ends. A few months later the family was back together.

In 1950 Leo went to Korea. Again the **urge**° to write, to create a reality of home for him, overtook me. I wrote every day for two years until

training in self-control

learning to form the letters of the alphabet

beginning

sure about the quality of

a lot of

(adj.) very small

strong desire

group of fruit trees

he came home. The letters focused on things I knew he would want to hear about: the state of the house he was building when he left, the **orchard°** he helped plant on Uncle Vic's farm, the mountains he loved, friends we both knew, relatives, and a host of the details that made up his life and ours together. . . .

What this early letter writing taught me was to focus on audience. Communication is not possible without common understandings, backgrounds, experiences . . . .

Comprehension. Answer the following questions.

1. How many members are there in the family?
2. Where are they? Why?
3. Why does the writer practice writing?
4. Describe the first letter the writer wrote to his sister.
5. What did he write about in the second letter to his sister?
6. Why did the writer write to his brother Leo?
7. What did he write about in his letters to Leo?
8. What did the writer learn from his early experiences of letter writing?

Discussion. Discuss these questions with your classmates or teacher.

1. Do you remember learning to write (in either your first or second language)? What do you remember about the experience?
2. Have you ever written regularly to someone? Who? What did you write about?
3. The writer says that "Communication is not possible without common understandings, backgrounds, experiences. . . ." Do you agree with him?
4. If you write to someone who has a different background or experience from yours, what do you need to do?

The Parts of a Paragraph

Most of the writing you do in college or at work consists of paragraphs. In academic writing, a **paragraph** is a small unit of writing that focuses on one idea. This one idea is explained and developed in the paragraph. The first line of each paragraph is indented. The indentation signals the beginning of a new paragraph.

A paragraph generally has three parts: **a topic sentence, support**, and a **conclusion**. The topic sentence tells the topic (what the paragraph is about) and the writer's attitude or idea about the topic. The supporting part of the paragraph explains, describes, or develops the main idea given in the topic sentence. The conclusion of the paragraph usually summarizes or comments on the main idea. The length of the paragraph depends upon the complexity of the topic.

Look at the three main parts in this paragraph written by a student. The topic sentence is in bold print and the concluding sentence is underlined. The rest of the paragraph is the support.

Parents can help their children be successful in school by encouraging them. Children usually enjoy playing games instead of studying their boring lessons, so parents have to take the responsibility to monitor their studying and to remind them to do their homework at home after school. Parents should also encourage their children to study by buying story books with pictures, or they can buy text books or tapes that help children learn to spell or read. The best way to encourage children to study efficiently is to reward them when they get an "A." As a child, I experienced this. My parents gave me a gift if I had studied well, and then I was very excited. <u>So, if parents really want their children to succeed in school, they need to pay attention to their children's studies and encourage them.</u>*

—Truong Dinh

The Topic Sentence

The **topic sentence** is the main-idea sentence. It is the most general and most important sentence of the paragraph. It tells the following:

the topic—what the paragraph is about
the controlling idea—the writer's attitude or idea about the topic

The **controlling idea** is a word or phrase that focuses or controls the information in the rest of the paragraph. The reader can ask questions about the controlling idea and expect to have them answered in the paragraph.

In the paragraph above, the topic sentence is the following:

Parents can help their children be successful in school by encouraging them.

The topic of the sentence is *how parents can help children succeed in school;* the controlling idea is *encouraging*. The reader might ask the following questions and expect the paragraph to answer them:

How can parents encourage their children?
What specific things should parents do to encourage their children?
How will this encouragement lead to success?

---

* In this book, you will read many paragraphs written by ESL students while they were in an ESL class. Most of the grammatical errors in the paragraphs have been corrected to make them easier to read and understand.

The topic sentence gives the writer's attitude, opinion, or idea about the topic. In it, the writer makes a judgement. Often, the topic sentence will include words like *helpful, easy, difficult, exciting, dangerous, disappointing, useful, encourage, deserve, protect, improve, forgive, value,* and so on.

ACTIVITY 1-1 Study the following topic sentences. Underline the topic and circle the controlling idea in each one. The first one is done as an example.

1. Receiving an F on my report card was a (humiliating) experience.

2. When I was a child, my grandfather's backyard was a magical place.

3. One reason I admire Nelson Mandela is that he never gave up.

4. The first step in learning how to do word processing is the hardest.

5. The greatest difference in education between the two countries is the number of subjects students must take.

Because a paragraph is a short piece of writing, the topic sentence for a paragraph must be precise. A topic sentence that is too broad and vague will be difficult to develop adequately in one paragraph. Look at this topic sentence:

Pollution is a problem.

There are many kinds of pollution and they each create a variety of problems. The writer should limit the topic to a particular kind of pollution and focus on a particular problem. Here the sentence is more focused:

The pollution of Lake Pontchartrain in New Orleans has caused problems for swimmers.

ACTIVITY 1-2 Study the following pairs of topic sentences. Circle the number of the better topic sentence in each pair. The first one is done as an example.

1. Divorce creates problems for parents and children.
2. When their parents divorce, children often feel insecure.

3. New Orleans is an interesting place to visit.
4. The French Quarter in New Orleans has a quaint, European charm.

5. Walking is good for your heart.
6. Exercise is good for you.

7. Computers are more important now than ever before.
8. Computers make revising an essay easy.

9. My parents have taught me to be persistent.
10. My parents have had a great influence on me.

The topic sentence can appear in a number of places in a paragraph. Often it is the first sentence of the paragraph. Putting the topic sentence at the beginning helps the writer to remember the controlling idea. It also helps the reader to focus quickly on the important information in the paragraph.

The topic sentence can also appear in the middle or at the end of the paragraph. It is possible for the topic sentence not to appear in the paragraph at all; it can be implied. In this case, the writer has the topic sentence in his or her mind and uses it to control the paragraph. If the writer uses an implied topic sentence, he or she must be sure that the reader can clearly understand the writer's attitude or controlling idea from the flow of ideas in the paragraph.

ACTIVITY 1-3 Study the following paragraphs. Write out the topic sentence for each paragraph. Underline the topic and circle the controlling idea in each topic sentence.

1. Ads on TV give consumers a lot of information. They let consumers know what products look like, how much they cost, and where they are available. For example, a Toyota dealer wants to sell the Toyota Camry. The dealer's ads will show the new Camry over and over again and tell the consumer that the Camry has power windows, six cylinders, etc. The ads may compare the Camry with the Mercedes. They may say that the Camry runs as well as the Mercedes but the Camry's price is much cheaper. The ads may also tell where to buy the Camry. It is only sold at the Toyota dealer, which is located on Lapalco Boulevard. When consumers see these ads, they think about all this information about the Camry. Then they can decide if it is the car they want.

   —*Huynh Tran*

   Topic Sentence: _____

   _____

2. The next time you go shopping at the Real Superstore, pay attention when the salesman is checking out items. You can see the price of each item coming up on the computer screen one at a time, and you can also hear the computer repeating the price. The only thing that the salesman has to do is just pass the items over the surface of the computer, and it takes care of the rest. Then, when the salesman finishes checking the items, the computer prints out a total list of all your items, including taxes. A salesman, depending on how fast he moves, can check out hundreds of items in eight to ten minutes. Thus, the computer has really speeded up the checkout process in stores.

   —*Diony Meunier*

   Topic Sentence: _____

   _____

3.   People can learn whatever language they want on Flatbush Avenue, the central street in Brooklyn, New York. On this street are many little stores, for example, Chinese, Cuban, Jamaican, Italian, Puerto Rican, American, and Haitian. This diversity of stores reflects the different ethnic backgrounds of the people living there. On this street, people can learn a new language because they interact with people of different nations. For example, I went to a store and one of the employees who looked Spanish asked me in my language, "Ou pa we sa ou vle." In Haitian Creole that means did I see anything I wanted. I was surprised to hear him speak my language, so I asked him where he had learned Creole. He said that Haitian people had taught him when they came into his store shopping. Another example is my uncle. One day I heard him speaking Spanish, and I asked him where he had learned it. He said, "Oh, from the Spanish people I know, on the street, and going into their stores." He said I could easily learn Spanish without any courses at school. Flatbush Avenue is the place to learn foreign languages.

—*Marie Rochelin*

Topic Sentence: _____

_____

Support

The **support** in a paragraph explains or develops the topic sentence. The supporting part can be narratives, details, facts, examples, explanation, or statistics. All of the support relates to the main idea stated in the topic sentence and shows why the topic sentence is true.

Here is a brief list of the support in the paragraph on page 7. Notice that all of the support explains ways that parents can encourage their children.

Topic Sentence:
   Parents can help their children be successful in school by encouraging them.
Support:
   1. Parents can encourage children by reminding them to do their homework.
   2. Parents can encourage children by buying them books and tapes to help them learn.
   3. Parents can encourage children by rewarding them.

ACTIVITY 1-4   Study the following paragraph. Write out the topic sentence. Underline the topic and circle the controlling idea. Then list the support.

The Internet is a very useful tool for college students. For example, students can learn about different cultures. They can have a friend in China and compare cultures using email. As a result, they can understand and appreciate other cultures better. If they have a math problem, they can easily find a tutor or help on the Internet. Students who want to learn a different language can find places where they can listen to tapes to simulate a teacher. If they have to do a research paper on a specific topic, all they have to do is go to the Internet and they will find the information instantly. The Internet is useful to college students in many ways.

—*Diana I. Robledo*

Topic Sentence: _____

_____

Support:

1. _____

_____

2. _____

_____

3. _____

_____

4. _____

_____

ACTIVITY 1-5   Following are some topic sentences. Write three possible sentences of support that could be included in a paragraph. Then, discuss your support with your teacher and classmates to determine if it relates to the main idea.

1. Topic Sentence: Parents can help their children succeed in school by offering financial support.

Support: _____

_____

Support: _____

_____

Support: _____

_____

2. Topic Sentence: Using a cell phone while driving is dangerous.

Support: _____

_____

Support: _____

_____

Support: _____

_____

3. Topic Sentence: Watching TV is a good way to learn spoken English.

Support: _____

_____

Support: _____

_____

Support: _____

_____

Conclusion

The **conclusion** of a paragraph summarizes or comments on the main idea. In a one-paragraph composition, the conclusion is one or two sentences. Often, the concluding sentences close the paragraph by returning to the main idea of the paragraph. They do this by repeating a key word or phrase from the topic sentence. Notice how the writer of the paragraph on page 7 repeats key words in his paragraph:

Topic Sentence:
   Parents can help their children be **successful** in school by **encouraging** them.

Concluding Sentence:
   So, if parents really want their children to **succeed** in school, they need to pay attention to their children's studies and **encourage** them.

Sometimes in the concluding sentences, the writer does not use the exact key words from the topic sentence but rephrases them, using other words that mean the same thing. This gives some variety to the paragraph. Notice how the key words in the topic sentence above could be rephrased:

Concluding Sentence:

Parents who want their children to **do their best** in school must **support** and pay attention to them.

In this concluding sentence, *do their best* means the same as *succeed* and *support* means the same as *encourage*.

ACTIVITY 1-6   Do the following activities.

1. Reread the paragraph in Activity 1-4, written by Diana I. Robledo, and do the following:
   a. Circle the key words the writer uses in both the topic sentence and conclusion.
   b. Rewrite the concluding sentence, rephrasing the key words.
2. Reread paragraph 3 in Activity 1-3, written by Marie Rochelin, and do the following:
   a. Circle the key words the writer uses in both the topic sentence and conclusion.
   b. Rewrite the concluding sentence, rephrasing the key words.

Title

A composition should have a **title**. The title introduces the reader to the composition, so it should give a clue to the main point of the composition. Usually, the title is a relevant word or phrase, not a complete sentence. All of the major words in the title are capitalized. The title should not have quotation marks (" ") around it.

Here are several possible titles for the paragraph on page 7:

Success in School
Helping Your Child Succeed in School
Encouraging Children to Succeed

ACTIVITY 1-7   Reread the paragraphs in Activity 1-3. Give each paragraph a title.

1. Title for paragraph 1: _____

2. Title for paragraph 2: _____

3. Title for paragraph 3: _____

Form

When you write a paragraph, follow these guidelines for the **form** of the paragraph.

1. Use 8½" × 11" notebook paper, with the holes on the left side.
2. Write your title on the first line by itself.
3. Indent the first line of the paragraph about an inch.
4. Leave a margin on the left and right sides of the paper.
5. Leave a space at the bottom and top of the paper.
6. For the copy you turn in to your teacher, write in ink on one side of the paper. If you can, type your paper.

The following example shows the form of a paragraph.

Helping Your Child Succeed in School

    Parents can help their children be successful in school by encouraging them. Children usually enjoy playing games instead of studying their boring lessons, so parents have to take the responsibility to observe their studying and to remind them to do their homework at home after school. Parents should also encourage their children to study by buying story books with pictures, or they can buy text books or tapes that help children learn to spell or read. The best way to encourage children to continue to study efficiently is to reward them when they get an "A." As a child, I experienced this. My parents gave me a gift if I had studied well, and then I was very excited. So, if parents really want their children to succeed in school, they need to pay attention to their children's studies and encourage them.

Truong Dinh

ACTIVITY 1-8   Write a paragraph, using one of the topic sentences in Activity 1-5. Use the support you discussed with your classmates. Write a concluding sentence and give your paragraph a title. Be sure to use appropriate paragraph form.

Unity

One characteristic of a good paragraph is **unity**. In a unified paragraph, all the sentences relate to the topic and develop the controlling idea. If a sentence or idea in a paragraph does not relate to the main idea, the paragraph lacks unity. The sentences that do not relate to the main idea should be taken out of the paragraph and perhaps developed in another paragraph. Look at the following topic sentence:

The French Quarter in New Orleans is a lively tourist spot.

The writer of this paragraph will want to show how lively the French Quarter is. He or she will want to tell all of the things a tourist can do there. Which of the following sentences will help to support this idea?

1. There are at least a hundred jazz clubs in the French Quarter.
2. You can always find clowns, jugglers, mimes, and street musicians there.
3. People can sit at sidewalk cafés and watch all kinds of people pass by.
4. The French Quarter is quiet in August because of the heat.

ACTIVITY 1-9   Read the following paragraphs. For each one, underline the topic sentence. Then, draw a line through any sentences that do not support the main idea in the topic sentence.

1.   The most obvious reason to recycle waste is to save resources. Paper companies can save trees if they collect old paper, like newspapers and computer paper, and make the used paper into new paper. Picking up all the trash paper along the road also makes the environment neat and clean. By saving trees, they save the earth's resources. Companies that make aluminum cans can also save resources. Since aluminum is a mineral that comes from the earth, there is a limited supply of it. Some day it will all be gone. So, if we recycle aluminum cans, we can use the same aluminum over and over again. In this way we conserve the earth's resources.

—*Mo Fung (Jacky) Chan*

2.   Mr. Thomas was the worst teacher I ever had. He taught general science in tenth grade. The reason he was so bad was that he tried to embarrass students. He would call on someone to answer even when he knew that person didn't know the answer to the question. Then, he would tease the person and say things like

"you're stupid," or "that was the easiest question I have." All of the students hated going to his class. Of course, Ms. Lewis, the history teacher, was pretty bad, too. I think Mr. Thomas is the reason I'm now a business major. I'm looking forward to a career as a CPA.

Coherence

Another important characteristic of a good paragraph is **coherence**. In a coherent paragraph, the ideas are arranged logically. The ideas and sentences are in an order that makes sense to the reader. If the ideas are logically arranged, the reader can easily follow the progression of ideas. He or she can quickly understand the main idea and follow the writer's thinking.

Sometimes a writer puts sentences in the wrong order. This often happens when the writer remembers something he or she wanted to say earlier in the paragraph but includes it in the wrong place. This results in an incoherent paragraph because the arrangement of ideas seems illogical to the reader.

Read this paragraph. Is it logically arranged? Can you find ideas that are out of order?

The French Quarter in New Orleans is a lively tourist spot. During the day, tourists can jostle with the crowd on Royal Street and hunt for bargains in the many **antique shops**° and art galleries. In them they can find anything from English furniture to Chinese porcelain to early American bone buttons. Or they can stop in one of the crowded T-shirt shops on Decatur Street to buy souvenirs. After a morning of shopping, they might want to have a snack of café au lait and beignets at the Café du Monde. At this noisy sidewalk café, they can sit for hours, listening to a jazz group and watching clowns and mimes entertain laughing children. The art galleries on Royal Street feature both local and international artists. During the evening, the French Quarter comes alive with its best known activity—jazz. There are hundreds of jazz clubs playing all different kinds of jazz—traditional jazz, hot jazz, cool jazz, the blues. Tourists can eat, drink, dance, and party until the sun rises and then start all over again.

stores that sell valuable old items such as furniture and jewelry

The paragraph has a logical arrangement; it starts with morning activities, goes through the day, and ends with evening activities. However, it has one sentence that is out of order. Can you suggest a better place for this sentence?

The art galleries on Royal Street feature both local and international artists.

ACTIVITY 1-10   Read the following paragraphs. In each one, one or more sentences is out of order. Rewrite the paragraphs to make them more coherent by putting the sentences in logical order.

1.   (1)One of the proudest moments of my childhood was the time I recited a long poem for the Christmas program at school. (2)When I was in elementary school, every year the school put on a program at Christmas time. (3)When I was about eight years old, the teacher asked me to memorize a very long poem. (4)I was really excited because I loved to memorize and to recite in front of a group. (5)I worked hard to learn the poem. (6)All the students memorized poems to recite and learned songs to sing as a group. (7)By the time the day came for the program, I had memorized the entire poem. (8)I still remember how nervous I was when the teacher called my name. (9)But I got up from my seat, walked in front of the audience, and recited the poem, just as I had learned it. (10)When the poem was over, everyone clapped. (11)The name of the poem was "The Night Before Christmas." (12)I felt so proud of myself. (13)Even though memorizing the poem was a lot of work, it was worth it to hear the applause that day.

2.   (1)To me, Nelson Mandela is a real hero. (2)The main reason I admire him is that he fought for equal rights in his country and didn't give up until he had achieved his goal. (3)His courage only landed him on Robbin Island, one of the toughest prisons in the world, where he was held for 26 years. (4)As a young man, he became a fighter for equal rights in South Africa, where he courageously resisted the South African government's policy of apartheid. (5)Even so, when he was in prison, he didn't give up the fight. (6)He continued to talk to the other prisoners and try to get publicity for his cause. (7)After he was released from prison in 1990, he quickly took over the leadership of the opposition party and pushed the government even harder for a government that would represent all South Africans. (8)Finally, in 1994, he was successful; he saw his dream fulfilled.

Grammar Review

The following grammar points will help you understand the next section. If you want to review them, turn to the pages listed below.

Cohesion

The reader will be able to follow a paragraph easily if the paragraph has a smooth flow. Smooth flow means that one sentence leads easily into the next sentence; the sentences are well-connected. This characteristic of a paragraph is called **cohesion**. There are a number of ways to increase the smooth flow of paragraphs. In the following chapters, you will study these methods of cohesion: repetition of ideas, pronoun consistency, and connecting words.

Cohesion: Connecting Words

Connecting words are words and phrases that show the relationship between ideas. They connect one idea to the next.

There are four kinds of connecting words. All of them can be used to connect sentences or clauses and to show the relationship of ideas. You will study them in detail in the following chapters in this book.

1. Key Words in Sentences

Key words are important signals that connect ideas. They are part of the structure of a sentence.

> **I remember the day** I met my future wife.
> **An example of** a hard-working student is Ali.

Because key words are part of the sentence structure, they have no particular punctuation.

You will study key words as they are appropriate in each chapter.

2. Coordinators

Coordinators connect two independent clauses to make one sentence.*

> I hid behind my mother, **and** I did not look at the teacher.
> I wanted to talk to her, **but** I was afraid.
> I could tell the teacher, **or** I could suffer in silence.
> The school was near my house, **so** it only took five minutes to walk there.

---

* If you do not know what independent and dependent clauses are, study them in the Grammar Review Section, pages 209–263.

Punctuation for coordinators with two independent clauses: a comma after the first clause.

For a complete list of coordinators, see page 210 in Appendix C-1.

3. Transitional Words

Transitional words (also called *conjunctive adverbs*) connect two independent clauses or two sentences.

With independent clauses:

During my last holiday I had to study for exams; **therefore**, I couldn't go camping.
I studied hard; **however**, I made time to see my friends.

Punctuation for transitional words with two independent clauses: a semicolon after the first clause and a comma after the transitional word.

With two sentences:

Abidjan is one of the largest cities in west Africa. **Moreover**, it has many modern office buildings.
It has an excellent port. **Therefore**, it is a center for importing and exporting.

Punctuation for transitional words with two sentences: a period after the first sentence and a comma after the transitional word.

For a complete list of transitional words, see page 214 in Appendix C-1.

4. Subordinators

Subordinators connect a dependent clause and an independent clause to make one sentence.

When I was eight years old, I memorized a long poem.
It was a big problem **because** we had different attitudes about it.
Although I tried to talk to her, she just laughed at me.

Punctuation for subordinators with clauses: a comma after the dependent clause when it is before the independent clause. (There is no comma when the dependent clause is after the independent clause.)

For a complete list of subordinators, see page 216 in Appendix C-1.

For a complete summary of connecting words and their punctuation, see pages 218–219 in Appendix C-1.

ACTIVITY 1-11   In the following sentences, circle the connecting word or words. If the sentences need punctuation or capitalization, add it. The first one is done as an example.

1. (When) consumers see these ads, they think about all this information.
2. Because many grocery stores use computers, checking out is fast.
3. I was surprised to hear him speak my language so I asked him where he had learned Creole.
4. When the poem was over everyone clapped.
5. On this street, people can learn a new language for example my uncle learned Spanish by talking with Spanish people.
6. One day I heard him speaking Spanish and I asked him where he had learned it.
7. The dealer's ads will show the Camry over and over again and tell the consumer that the Camry has power windows and six cylinders.
8. He would call on someone who didn't know the answer then he would tease that person.
9. Although I knew the poem by heart I was still nervous.

ACTIVITY 1-12   Write a sentence or two using each of the connecting words given. Use correct punctuation. The first is done as an example.

1. Credit cards are useful. You don't have to carry cash.
   so   <u>You don't have to carry cash, so credit cards are useful.</u>

   therefore _____

   because _____

2. You can use them in the grocery store. You can buy plane tickets with them.

   moreover _____

   and _____

3. They are easy to use. You have to pay the bill at the end of the month.

   however _____

   but _____

   although _____

Writing a Paragraph

You have just studied the characteristics of a paragraph. Now it is time to think about the process of writing a paragraph. As you write paragraphs and essays in this book, you will go through certain steps that will help you write well-focused and well-developed paragraphs. In this section, you will study a general approach to writing a paragraph that you can use in each of the following chapters.

Considering Audience

In writing, **audience** means the people who will read your piece of writing. If you know the background and interests of your audience, you can focus your writing to that audience more effectively. Think about the reading at the beginning of the chapter, in which Michael Flanigan tells about learning to write. In the experiences he relates, how did he focus his writing to his audience?

In your writing, you must be concerned about your audience. For example, if you are going to write about an interesting tourist spot in your country, you must consider what your audience may or may not know about your country. If you are writing for a newspaper to be published in your country, you may assume your readers are familiar with the place. However, if you are writing for an ESL class in this country, your readers may not know much about your country, so you will need to give some background information.

As you write in this class, your teacher may ask you to choose a particular audience or to direct your writing to your teacher and classmates. In either case, think about the following when you consider your audience:

1. Who is going to read this piece of writing?
2. What does my audience know (or not know) about my topic?
3. What background information about my topic will my audience need to know?
4. What will my audience find interesting?
5. What is the main point I want my audience to understand?
6. How can I best get my audience to understand my point?

Getting Ideas

Sometimes your teacher will give you a topic; sometimes you must decide on your own. In either case, you must get some ideas about the topic. These ideas will help you narrow your topic, decide on a controlling idea, and develop enough support. So getting ideas is an important step in writing your paragraph.

There are a number of strategies you can use to get ideas about your topic. All of them involve two things: thinking about the topic and writing about the topic. Together, thinking and writing will help you shape and develop ideas. (Strategies for Getting Ideas are listed in Appendix B, pages 204–208.)

Narrowing the Topic

When you first get your topic for writing, it will probably be a broad subject like education, sports, or an important place, person, or decision in your life. You need to think about this broad subject and narrow it down to a topic you can write about in one paragraph.

One strategy for getting ideas is **brainstorming**. To brainstorm, first write your subject on a piece of paper. It could be a word, a phrase, or a question. Think about your subject and write down any ideas that come to mind. Write quickly without evaluating your ideas. After you have listed as many ideas as you can, read over your list. Narrow your topic by circling ideas you might want to use in your paragraph.

Here is an example of brainstorming.

An Interesting Place in My Country

Washington, DC—monuments
                    —museums
New York—Broadway
San Francisco—
Rocky Mountains—Colorado
                    —Grand Canyon
New Orleans—French Quarter
                    —zoo
                    —aquarium
Florida—Disney World

In this brainstorming, the writer has listed a number of places she thinks is interesting and then circled the one she wants to write about.

ACTIVITY 1-13   Following are some broad topics. Choose one of the subjects, brainstorm, and narrow it down.

1. An interesting tourist spot
2. An important decision
3. Learning a second language
4. Computers
5. Shopping
6. Parents
7. A friend

Deciding on a Controlling Idea

Once you have narrowed your topic, you will need to get more ideas about it in order to focus on a controlling idea. You may want to brainstorm again or use another one of the strategies listed in Appendix B. Write as much as you can and think about the main point you want to make. The writer above chose the French Quarter in New Orleans as a topic and then brainstormed a second time. Here is an example of a second brainstorming to develop more ideas about the topic.

The French Quarter

interesting	Café du Monde—green and white awning
historic	—people watching
lots of people	—drinking café au lait
exciting	—eating beignets
(lively)	—saxophone player
noisy	famous restaurants—Galatoire's
jazz clubs	Jackson Square —statue of Andrew Jackson
Bourbon Street	—flower gardens
Royal Street—antiques	—iron benches under shade trees
—art galleries	
narrow streets—brick	
European feeling—quaint	
architecture—iron railings	
—long windows	

Notice that the writer has listed a lot of ideas. She has circled the one idea that she wants to use as a controlling idea for the paragraph.

ACTIVITY 1-14   Use the topic you narrowed down in Activity 1-13 and brainstorm again. After you have finished brainstorming, choose a controlling idea and write a topic sentence.

Choosing Support

Once you have decided on a controlling idea, you need to look again at the brainstorming notes to find support for your idea. You may find all the support you need, or you may need to add to your notes. To get more ideas, brainstorm again or use another one of the strategies listed in Appendix B. You will probably not use all of the notes in your brainstorming; choose only those ideas that support your controlling idea and leave the rest.

Next, organize your notes in a logical way. Make a list of your support. Here is a list of support for the paragraph on the French Quarter.

Topic Sentence: The French Quarter in New Orleans is a lively tourist spot.

Support: Daytime—activities
          Royal Street
            antique shops
              English furniture
              Chinese porcelain
              early American bone buttons
           art galleries—local/international artists

> Decatur Street
>   T-shirt shops—souvenirs
> Café du Monde
>   snack—café au lait and beignets
>   sit and watch the people
>   jazz group
>   clowns and mimes
>   other people passing by
> At night—comes alive
>   jazz—all kinds
>   traditional
>   hot
>   cool
>   the blues
>   have a good time

Compare this organized list of support with the brainstorming notes on pages 22 and 23. Circle the ideas the writer has used from the brainstorming. Notice the ideas the writer did not use. Why didn't she use them?

Once you have organized your notes, write a first draft of your paragraph.

ACTIVITY 1-15   Choose support from your brainstorming notes to support the topic sentence you developed in Activity 1-14. Organize your support into a list.

Topic Sentence: _____

_____

Support: _____

_____

_____

_____

_____

ACTIVITY 1-16   Write the paragraph you have developed from your brainstorming.

Revising

After you have written a first draft of your paragraph, you will want to **revise** it. To revise means to think about your paragraph again and make changes. When you revise, you will want to sharpen your focus and make sure that your reader can follow your ideas. You will use the Revising Checklist in each chapter to evaluate your paragraph.

It is also a good idea to get a classmate to read your paragraph and give you feedback. As your audience, your classmates can tell you if they understand the main idea of the paper and if the paper is interesting.

If you want to get a classmate's feedback on your paper, exchange your paragraph with a partner. Use the questions in the Paragraph Guidelines in each chapter to evaluate each other's papers. When you have done that, discuss your comments with your partner. Using your partner's suggestions, revise your paper.

ACTIVITY 1-17   Following is a paragraph written by a student. Evaluate it using the questions in the Paragraph Guidelines below.

Language is one of the most difficult things foreigners face in another country. They find it difficult to ask for directions to hospitals and hotels, but they will get used to it after two or three months. Another thing is the food. Foreigners find different food from what they usually eat. This aspect is more difficult for people who don't know how to cook. For example, when I arrived in the U.S.A., I found that people eat pork, while in my country we never eat it. I also found strange food which I liked very much.

—*Ali Al-Ghamdi*

Paragraph Guidelines

1. Write out the topic sentence.
2. Underline the topic and circle the controlling idea.
3. Summarize the support in one or two sentences. That is, tell the support in your own words.
4. Is there a clear, focused topic sentence and controlling idea?
5. Do all of the sentences support the controlling idea?
6. Is the paragraph organized in a logical way?
7. What part of the paragraph do you like the most?
8. Is there any part that you do not understand?

ACTIVITY 1-18   Evaluate the paragraph you wrote in Activity 1-16 in one of the following ways and then revise it.

A. Ask a partner to evaluate the paragraph using the Paragraph Guidelines.
B. Evaluate the paragraph yourself using the Revising Checklist.

Revising Checklist

1. Is the topic narrowed down enough?
2. Do you have a topic sentence?
3. Do you have a clear, focused controlling idea?
4. Do all of the sentences support the controlling idea?
5. Is the paragraph organized in a logical way?
6. Is the paragraph interesting?

Using the Internet

 The Internet has a lot of resources that can help you learn English in a new way. In the chapters that follow, you will use the Internet to help you in your writing.

INTERNET ACTIVITY   If you want help with understanding topic sentences, paragraph support, unity, coherence, or cohesion, you can go to an Online Writing Lab, an OWL. Online Writing Labs give advice and information about writing and grammar. Find out if your school has an OWL. If it does not, use a search engine such as Google, Yahoo!, or Excite and do a keyword search for "online writing labs." You could also visit the OWL at Purdue University at http://owl.english .purdue.edu/.

Keeping a Journal

A journal is a notebook in which you can write about anything. You can write about your thoughts, ideas, dreams, frustrations, studies, and friends. It is a place where you can reflect on your life and make observations about the world around you. You can also reflect on writing—on how you write, what is easy, and what is hard.

In this course, you will use your journal to write on topics during class time. You should also use your journal to write about your own topics at home. Each chapter has some suggestions for topics to write about.

Because your journal is a place for you to write freely, your teacher will not grade it or mark grammatical errors. However, she or he may collect it and respond to what you have written.

Your teacher will give you particular instructions about the kind of journal you should have and how much writing you should do. The most important thing is to write about topics you care about and to write regularly.

Here are several topics for your first journal entry. Write at least one page.

1. Do you remember learning to write? Write about what you remember from that experience.
2. Write about a time when you wrote something you were proud of.
3. How do you feel when you write in English? Why?
4. How do you feel when you write in your first language? Do you enjoy it?
5. Have you ever written regularly to someone? Write about that experience.
6. Write about the most interesting thing you learned in this chapter.

Chapter ② Narrating

Theme

Memorable Events

Goals

Writing

To write a paragraph narrating a memorable event

To write a topic sentence with a strong controlling idea

To choose an incident to support the main point

> To organize the events of the incident using chronological order

> To improve cohesion by using connecting words for narration

To choose an interesting point of view

Reading

To read about and reflect on other writers' memorable events and personal discoveries

Grammar

To review past tenses for narrating and simple present tense for explaining

To review used to/would

To review adverbial clauses of time

Getting Started

Journal Writing: A Memorable Event

Think about an event or incident in your past that you remember well. In your journal, write about this incident. Answer the following questions:

1. Where did the incident take place?
2. When did the incident happen?
3. Who were the people involved?
4. What happened?
5. How did you feel about the incident?
6. Why was this incident memorable or important?

Discussion. Tell your classmates or teacher about the incident you have chosen.

CNN® Video Activity: Adult Illiteracy

Many adults in the United States, including some high school graduates, cannot read and write well. This video clip tells the story of Enrique Ramirez and other adults who have overcome their problems with reading.

Before you watch the video, discuss these questions with your classmates or teacher.

1. How many adults in the United States do you think are unable to read and write?
2. What kinds of problems do illiterate adults face in daily life?
3. What can illiterate adults do to help themselves learn to read?

Understanding the Video

Comprehension. Read the following questions before you watch the video. After you watch the video, answer the questions.

1. How did Enrique Ramirez feel when he was unable to read a story to his son?
2. What percentage of high school graduates in the United States cannot read and write well?
3. Why is going to the grocery store sometimes a frightening experience for illiterate people?
4. What class does Enrique Ramirez now teach?
5. Are reading problems limited to certain cultural groups?
6. How does Enrique Ramirez feel now about asking his son for help?
7. What is the lesson that the video ends with?

Discussion. After you watch the video, discuss these questions with your class-mates or teacher.

1. Why are many adults in the United States unable to read and write?
2. What kinds of work are illiterate people able/unable to do? Do you know any-one illiterate? How does he or she cope without reading?
3. Does illiteracy cause other social problems? What are they?
4. Why is it important for parents to know how to read?

Reading

Discuss these questions with your classmates or teacher.

1. Look at the map in Appendix A, pages 202–203. Find Southeast Asia and draw in the country of Vietnam. What do you know about this country?
2. What do you think is the relationship between the two boys in the pictures below?
3. What do you think is happening in the pictures?
4. Does the boys' relationship change? How?

Reading

My Fault
by Hoang Vo

This essay was written by Hoang Vo when he was studying electrical engineering at the University of New Orleans. He wrote this essay when he was a student in an ESL class.

I remember vividly the day I made a big mistake regarding one of my friends. I was eleven years old, in the fifth grade, and I went to a school in the country. The school, which was very small and poor, had about twenty classrooms.

I and my friend, who became acquainted with me about a year before, studied in the same classroom. We quickly became familiar and even more friendly than before. When either of us did not understand something, we would ask each other to clear up our questions.

Our classroom had a shelf which was made of wood and painted brown. The teacher used it to place **miscellaneous**° things on. Among those things, she especially liked a pink flower vase which was made of pottery. One time, she told the students that her mother had given her this flower vase a long time ago when she had gone to visit her mother in town.

One day, when we were waiting for the teacher, my friend and I went to the shelf to look at the objects on it. We saw a toy car on top of the shelf and because it was too high to reach, my friend grabbed the edge of the shelf with his right hand and started to climb up. Suddenly his left hand **collided with**° the flower vase. It fell on the floor with a little dry sound; the flower vase was broken into pieces.

Before we could think of what to do next, the teacher appeared in the door. We ran back to our seats and we told nobody what had happened. The teacher quickly noticed the pieces of the broken vase on the floor. She was **stunned**° for a moment. Then she slowly turned her face to the class and asked in a trembling voice who had broken the vase.

Nobody answered her question. After a moment of silence, she said in an angry voice that if anybody had seen someone break the flower vase and did not willingly point out the **culprit,**° then when she found out he would get the same punishment as the one who broke the vase. When I heard those words, I became afraid of the punishment if I kept silent. I stood up, pointed my finger at my friend, and said that he had broken the vase. I slumped down in my chair as if I had just thrown a

several different

hit, struck

too upset to speak

guilty person

selfishness

burden from my shoulder, but now, because of my **egotism,**° this burden was transferred to my friend. He was flogged with a ruler five times on his palm.

Maybe my friend will forgive me for what I did to him, but I will never forget my fault. All these years later, I always promise myself that I will never do that to my friends again; I will never let my friends think of me as a mean person.

Comprehension. Answer the following questions.

1. Where did the incident take place?
2. When did the incident happen?
3. Who were the people involved?
4. What happened in this incident?
5. How did the writer feel about it?
6. What effect did this incident have on the writer's life?
7. Write five or six sentences telling the story to someone who has not read it. Tell the story in your own words.

Discussion. Discuss these questions with your classmates or teacher.

1. What do you think about the writer's action of telling the teacher who broke the vase? Did he do the right thing? Was it a typical action for a schoolboy?
2. Was the writer able to reflect on and learn from this incident?
3. Have you ever done something because you were afraid and then regretted it later? Tell about the incident.
4. Have you ever done something from which you learned a lesson?

NOTE: If you want to read about other memorable events, read the following:

Mary Kay Mackin's story of winning a contest on pages 46–47
Orestes Lorenzo's story of his escape from Cuba on page 48–49

Preparing to Write

Focusing on a Main Point

To narrate is to tell a story or describe an incident. In academic writing, the writer may use an incident to **illustrate a point**. For example, if you are writing a paper about homelessness, you might tell the story of a homeless person. In the world of work, a doctor, lawyer, or businessperson may write a narrative as a record of an interview or incident.

The topic sentence for a narrative paragraph should give the topic (the event the writer is telling about) and the controlling idea (the writer's attitude or feeling about the event). A strong controlling idea helps to focus the paragraph and helps the reader understand the writer's purpose for writing the paragraph. Look at the topic sentences below. Which one has a clearer controlling idea?

I spent my vacation at Disney world.
My vacation at Disney world was a disappointment.

ACTIVITY 2-1   Read the following paragraphs written by students. For each one, write a topic sentence with a clear controlling idea. The first one is done as an example.

1. *When I was charged with a crime I didn't commit, I was very worried.*

After coming home from school one day, I had to take my son to the doctor because he had a high fever. Then I quickly drove to the Superstore to buy medicine for him and came home. Only fifteen minutes after I got home, a policeman with a serious face and a gun in his holster appeared at my door to ask me some questions about an accident I wasn't aware of. He carefully inspected my car and beckoned me to get into his police car, which was parked in front of the house. Looking back towards the house, I saw my daughter, my niece, and my old parents anxiously watching me through the window. I slowly got into the police car. By that time, I felt nearly unconscious and thought maybe I was going to be sent to jail. I wanted to know which accident I was supposedly involved in, so I asked the policeman. He looked at me suspiciously and told me that I had hit the car next to mine while I was backing out of the parking lot in front of the doctor's office. Apparently, while I was driving away, the driver, who said that I had hit his car, had copied my license plate number and called the police. After collecting information about the event, the policeman charged me with a hit and run accident, and told me to appear in court the following month on the fifteenth. I worried about this for the next month. When I went to court, I had strong evidence that I was not guilty, so the judge ruled that I was innocent and dropped the charge against me. As soon as I found out that I wasn't convicted, I exhaled slowly and felt relieved because a problem had been lifted from my mind. I thanked God a million times.

—Bachvan Doan

2. _____

   _____ .

   One day my friend Dax called me and talked for about an hour. I had known Dax for about four years and thought he was a nice, honest guy. He called again the next day and told me about his problem. He had lent his car to his friend Paco, who had an accident with it and then lied to Dax about what happened. When Dax tried to collect the insurance, he lied to the insurance company, saying that he was driving the car. The insurance company refused to pay to fix the car and decided to sue Dax for lying. Dax had to pay to fix the car himself and he had to get a lawyer to help with the case. Within a month, Dax had spent four thousand dollars. After I heard Dax's story, I felt sorry for him. Even though I believe that money and friendship don't go together, I agreed to lend Dax two hundred dollars. He promised that he would pay me at the end of the month. At the end of the month, he called and said he didn't have the money. That situation continued for six months. After that, I gave up and didn't ask him for the money. Then, he had the nerve to call me and ask for another loan. I was amazed. I refused and told him I didn't have any money left. He said I was greedy. I told him he was a cheat and hung up the phone. Even though I felt sad to lose a friend over money, I think it was better to find out now than later.

   —*Jill Zea*

3. _____

   _____ .

   In our religion, boys must not see girls when they become adults. However, when a man wants to get married, he has the right to see the girl he is going to marry. A particular girl moved to my city when I was sixteen years old, so I hadn't seen her before. I told my mother that I wanted to marry this girl and my mother agreed. After two weeks, my mother talked to the girl's mother and she agreed. Three days later, I went with my parents to visit the girl's parents and see the girl. I wore my best clothes. My father and I sat with her father and brother. We drank tea and we talked about some business. Then they gave me permission to enter the room. My heart started beating faster and faster; I started sweating. I went to the mirror and made sure I looked okay. I started walking into the room where she sat with her mother and my mother. I entered the door and saw my mother, who was waiting for me. She grasped my hand and sat me beside the girl. I sat and looked out of the corner of my eyes, trying to get a glimpse of her. Suddenly my mother took a hold of my head and forced me to look at her. She was very pretty. I didn't think she would be that pretty. I didn't talk to her because she was shy. I stayed for ten minutes or more and then I left.

—*Ali Al-Ghamdi*

4. _____

_____ .

It was a beautiful morning in Moscow, Monday, August 19, 1991. I woke up in a very good mood, looked out of the window and determined that it was going to be a great day. I called my friend, who was to be my future wife. Her roommate picked up the phone and asked me if I knew what had happened last night. I said no. Then she told me there had been a coup. I did not believe her, so I turned on the TV. Since there was a symphony orchestra playing the same music on all channels, I knew something had happened. I turned on the radio and found a channel with a government announcement. The radio said that Gorbachev was sick and the situation in the country dictated that strong people should take over the government. I was so nervous that I almost cried. I didn't know what to do. By the end of the day, in a metro station, I found a paper pasted to the wall. The paper said that Boris Yeltzin had not been arrested as I thought, and he was calling men to the parliament building to protect democracy. I went there and stayed there for two nights at the barricades. I knew that it was dangerous, but I also knew that I didn't want to live in a country with a totalitarian regime anymore.

—*Ditmar Hospital*

ACTIVITY 2-2   Following are several events you have probably experienced. Think about a particular incident that you experienced during each event. Then name the incident and tell your attitude or feeling about it.

Example: a vacation or trip

NAME OF THE INCIDENT	ATTITUDE
the time our car broke down	frightened

1. a vacation or trip
2. a party
3. a test in a particular school subject

4. a game you participated in
5. a family celebration

Supporting the Main Point with an Incident

Focusing on a Particular Incident

In narrative writing, the writer focuses on a particular incident to support the main point. The incident consists of events that are linked in time. All of the events given should support the controlling idea. The writer also includes words and details that support the controlling idea. Look at this analysis of the first paragraph in Activity 2-1.

FOCUSING ON AN INCIDENT
Controlling Idea: Worried

EVENTS	DETAILS
I came home from school	
I took my son to the doctor	he had a high fever
I went to the Superstore for medicine	I drove quickly
I came home	
a policeman came to my door	with a serious face and gun
he inspected my car	
he beckoned me to get into the police car	
I looked at my family	anxiously watching me
I got into the police car	slowly
	I felt nearly unconscious
	I thought I might go to jail
I asked the policeman about the accident	he looked at me suspiciously
he told me I had hit a car at the doctor's office	
the policeman charged me with a hit and run accident	I worried about this for the next month
I went to court and presented evidence	
I was found not guilty	I exhaled slowly and felt relieved
	a problem had been lifted from my mind
	I thanked God a million times

ACTIVITY 2-3   Look again at the paragraphs in Activity 2-1. Choose paragraph 2, 3, or 4 and analyze it on a separate sheet of paper. Use the analysis in Activity 2-2 as an example.

1. Write the controlling idea at the top of the paper.
2. On the left side of the paper, make a list of the events.
3. On the right side, make a list of the words and details that support the controlling idea.

ACTIVITY 2-4   Choose one of the incidents you listed in Activity 2-2 and write the following on a piece of paper.

1. Write the controlling idea at the top.
2. On the left side of the paper, make a list of the events in the incident.
3. On the right side, make a list of words and details you could use to support the controlling idea.

Giving Background Information

Sometimes it is necessary for the writer to give background information. The background information provides a context for the incident. It helps the reader to understand the incident. In the following paragraph, the background information is in bold print.

When I Refused To Listen to My Parents

Once I felt sorry that I didn't listen to my parents' advice. **In my country, Saudi Arabia, I used to go out with my brother, friends, or relatives to popular places on the weekends. I used to study from Saturday to Wednesday. Then the weekend is from Wednesday night to Friday.** One Wednesday, after working hard at school, I had to do something. In the evening, I washed my father's car and called some of my friends to go out that night to King Fahad Park. At nine o'clock, I told my parents but they didn't want me to go. They said it was too late, but I didn't listen to them. I just went out and drove to my friends' house to pick them up. While we were driving on the main road in the park, there was another car in the middle lane. Suddenly, the driver of that car turned into my lane without giving a signal. I switched on the bright lights, pounded on the horn, and stepped on the brakes, but nothing worked. The other car forced me to hit the wall on the side of the main road. When the car stopped, my friends and I got out. It was a miracle that nobody was hurt. My father's car was in bad condition; it was like a sandwich. At that moment, I remembered my parents' words when they didn't want me to go out. Later, the police came, and I arranged with a garage to fix my father's car. After three days, I told my father about everything. First, he wanted to know if anyone was hurt. Then, he told me to be careful next time and scolded me. <u>Next time, I will take my parents' advice, so that I will not feel sorry again. If they say something to me, it is for my advantage.</u>

—Hussein Al-Qahtani

Explaining the Main Point

Sometimes, the writer explains or analyzes the story. The writer may tell the significance or meaning of the story or make a comment about it. Often he or she explains the story from the present perspective. In the paragraph above, the writer's comment on the story is underlined.

ACTIVITY 2-5   Look at the lists you made in Activity 2-4. For the same incident, do the following.

1. List the necessary background information.
2. Write several sentences explaining the main point.

Organizing by Chronological Order

In telling a narrative, a writer organizes the events in the story according to time. This organizational pattern is called **chronological order.** The writer gives the topic sentence, necessary background information, the story itself, and an explanation of the point. Often, these parts are arranged as follows:

Topic Sentence
Background Information
Story
Explanation or Comment

Topic Sentence
Background Information
Story
Explanation or comment

ACTIVITY 2-6   Write the paragraph you worked on in Activity 2-5.

ACTIVITY 2-7   The following paragraph has some problems. What suggestions can you make to help the writer improve the paragraph? Read the paragraph and answer the questions that follow.

Two months ago my family and I went to Slidell to celebrate my nephew's birthday. My two daughters were so happy. They like to go to my nephew's house because he has a lot of toys. That Sunday it was raining. My husband was driving the car. He hadn't slept very well the night before because he had to study very hard for a test on Monday. There was a brown car in front of us, and I was talking with my husband when this car stopped suddenly. The pavement was very slippery because of the rain, so we couldn't stop and the car crashed. Everybody in the car was scared. My two daughters, who were sitting in the back seat, were crying. The first thing that came to my mind was them. Fortunately none of us had any injuries. When I looked at my husband, his face was white. I think he was really scared for the children too. Two hours after the accident happened, a policeman came and took information about the accident. He asked my husband and the other driver, who wasn't hurt, for their driver's licenses and insurance cards. The policeman was very nice. He said that my husband was guilty because he was supposed to stop. The insurance company paid everything for both cars. It wasn't a big accident but we decided to come back home and rest. Two days later we went to the doctor's office and he told us that our children were fine.

—*Nora Maldonado*

1. Write out the topic sentence and circle the controlling idea.
2. List any background information.
3. Briefly summarize the incident. That is, write several sentences telling what happened in your own words.
4. Briefly summarize the writer's explanation of her main point.
5. Does the paragraph have a clear topic sentence and controlling idea?
6. Is the paragraph unified? Do all of the sentences support the controlling idea?
7. Are the events in the incident in chronological order?
8. What part of the paragraph did you enjoy the most?
9. What part would you like to know more about?

Writing

Writing Assignment 1: Narrative

Now you are going to write a paragraph narrating an incident.

1. PREPARE TO WRITE.

   A. First, think about an incident that you would like to tell about. You may choose one of the topics listed below.

      A Lesson Learned

         A time when you confronted authority

         A time when you took responsibility

         A time when you had to deliver bad news

         A time when you had to repay a debt

      An Act of Generosity

      Firsts

         Your first day at school

         The first time you met someone who became important to you

         Your first performance

      Memorable Moments

         An important moment in your childhood

         A moment of great insight or understanding

         A difficult moment

         A humorous experience

   B. Get ideas about your incident by making a list of the events in your story. (See Appendix B, page 204, for an explanation and example of making a list, or review page 36 in this chapter.)

   C. Read over your list.

   D. Decide on your main point. Write a topic sentence with a clear controlling idea.

   E. Look again at the list of events. Circle those that are relevant to your main idea.

   F. Next to the events you are going to use, write words and details that will help support your main point.

   G. Decide what background information you will need to include.

   H. Write some sentences analyzing or explaining your main point.

I. Organize your paragraph using chronological order.

2. WRITE THE PARAGRAPH.

Remember your audience. Make your story interesting for the reader.

3. REVISE THE PARAGRAPH.

A. Ask a partner to evaluate your paragraph using the Paragraph Guidelines, or do it yourself using the Revising Checklist.

B. Revise your paragraph.

Paragraph Guidelines

1. Write out the topic sentence and circle the controlling idea.
2. List any background information.
3. Briefly summarize the incident. That is, write several sentences telling what happened in your own words.
4. Briefly summarize the explanation.
5. Does the writer have a clear topic sentence and controlling idea?
6. Do all of the sentences support the controlling idea?
7. Are the events in the incident in chronological order?
8. What part of the paragraph did you enjoy the most?
9. What part would you like to know more about?

Revising Checklist

1. Do you tell a story or incident?
2. Do you have a clear topic sentence?
3. Does the topic sentence have a clear, focused controlling idea?
4. Do all of the sentences support the controlling idea?
5. Are the events in the incident in chronological order?
6. Is the paragraph interesting?

Using Language Effectively

Cohesion: Connecting Words for Narration

In narration, the writer needs to show the relationship of events in time. The writer can make the time clear by using either key words that are prepositional phrases telling **when** or subordinators in adverbial clauses of time.*

---

* If you need to review adverbial clauses of time, see the Grammar Review, pages 225–226.

WORDS TO INDICATE TIME RELATIONSHIPS

KEY WORDS	SUBORDINATORS
after (a moment)	while
at (ten o'clock)	when
at noon	as
by (ten o'clock)	whenever
by that time	before
by then	after
during (the morning)	until
during that time	as soon as
from (six o'clock) to (ten o'clock)	the moment that
from then on	once
in (May)	
in (1994)	
on (Saturday)	
one (day, time)	
(three days) later	
until (six o'clock)	
until then	

Examples

I used to study from **Saturday to Wednesday.**

After a moment of silence, she asked who had broken the vase.

Examples

While I was driving away, the driver copied my license plate number.

When we got to school, I changed my mind.

Before we could think of what to do next, the teacher appeared in the door.

We were friends **until** I told the teacher about the vase.

As soon as I found out I wasn't convicted, I exhaled slowly.

The moment that I saw her I thought she was pretty.

In addition to time relationships, the reader must also know the sequence of events—what happened first, second, and so forth.

WORDS TO INDICATE SEQUENCE

TRANSITIONAL WORDS

---

first, second, etc.

next

later

suddenly

then

last

finally

now

Examples

First I called my friend. Then I turned on the radio.

First he wanted to know if anyone was hurt. **Then** he scolded me.

If the writer tells the events of the story in chronological order, the writer might not use many transitional words because the sequence of events is clear. In this case, the writer may use key words and subordinators to set the scene or to improve the flow of the sentences.

ACTIVITY 2-8   Read the following narrative and underline the connecting words.

When I started to work here in New Orleans, something really funny happened to me. My mother got me a job at the Marriott Hotel as a cocktail waitress. I was really nervous because I had never worked before. I trained for two days, but I didn't speak English at all except for one or two expressions. I tried to memorize the keys of the cash register but that was the only thing I could do. When my training was over, I was supposed to start on my own. From that moment it was a terrible start. Finally, I had my first customer. I went to the table and I said, "Hello, how you doing? Can I get you something?" The lady said, "Yes, I would like a glass of water and a **grasshopper.**"° I went to the bar, but I was afraid to pronounce the word "grasshopper," so I just got the glass of water. Then, I went to the table, and said, "Sorry, we don't have it." That lady started talking wildly. I realized something was wrong, so I said, "I'm sorry." I went back to the bar, asked the bartender for a grasshopper, and she fixed it for me. Now I laugh when I think about my fear.

a kind of drink

—*Saira Rodriguez*

Grammar Review

The following grammar points will help you write narration. If you want to review them, turn to the pages listed below.

Verb Tenses   Page 221
  Past Tenses for Narrating   Page 221
  Present Tense for Explaining Page 223
Used To and *Would*   Page 225
Adverbial Clauses of Time   Page 225

Using the Internet

 INTERNET ACTIVITY   Many Web sites give information about famous people. Use a search engine such as Google, Yahoo!, or Excite to find information about a famous person. Look for a particular incident in that person's life and do the following.

1. On a separate sheet of paper, write some notes about the incident.
   a. Write out the main point of the incident.
   b. Make a list of the events in the incident.
   c. Write an explanation or comment about the incident.
2. Using your notes, explain the incident to a partner or your classmates and teacher. In speaking, use the past tense, connecting words to indicate time relationships and sequence, and adverbial clauses of time.

3. Your teacher may ask you to write a paragraph about the incident.

Preparing to Write

Choosing a Point of View

The writer must choose a point of view. The point of view is the eye the writer looks through to see the events of the story. The writer can tell the story from his or her point of view or from the point of view of another person.

Reread the paragraph "When I Refused To Listen to My Parents" on pages 37–38. Notice that the writer tells the story from his own point of view. Can you imagine the story from the point of view of one of the other people? How did the writer's mother or father see this incident? How did it appear to one of his friends, the driver of the other car, the policeman, or the car mechanic? Since you were not part of the story, you cannot be sure, but you can imagine what happened. Perhaps this is how the writer's father saw the incident.

I will never forget the time my son, Hussein, learned a valuable lesson. One Wednesday night around nine o'clock I was eating dinner when he came in the room to talk to me. He seemed happy and excited. He wanted to go out with his friends to King Fahad Park and wanted to use my car. I told him that it was too late and that he should wait until the next day. Then he could go with my permission. He didn't say anything but just turned and left the room. I could tell that he was angry. I worried about this incident until I went to bed, but didn't think about it again until several days later. Then, again at dinnertime, Hussein came to see me. He looked scared and concerned. He told me that on the previous Wednesday night he had taken my car and had had an accident with it. He apologized and said that he was very sorry. My heart stopped. I was afraid someone had been hurt or, even worse, killed. He assured me that everyone was fine, and I was relieved. Then, however, I realized that he had disobeyed me and done something really foolish. I wanted him to learn a lesson from this. I became angry and scolded him. I told him he needed to be careful and not put himself or other people in danger. He looked very serious and sorry for what he had done. I think he understood what I said and became a more mature person that night.

ACTIVITY 2-9   Choose a paragraph from Activity 2-1 or 2-7 or choose Hoang Vo's essay, "My Fault," on pages 31–32, and do the following.

1. Reread the paragraph and decide whose point of view the story is from.
2. Choose one of the other people in the story and imagine the story from that person's point of view. Decide on a controlling idea and make some notes. You may need to add details that are not in the paragraph.
3. Tell the story from that person's point of view to a partner.

Writing

Writing Assignment 2: Point of View

Now you are going to rewrite one of your paragraphs from a different point of view.

1. Prepare to write.

   A. Use the paragraph you wrote in Writing Assignment 1 or Activity 2-6.

   B. Choose one of the other people in the incident and imagine the story from that person's point of view.

   C. To help you imagine, freewrite. (See Appendix B, page 206, for an explanation and example of freewriting.)

   D. Decide on a controlling idea.

E. Write a topic sentence.

F. Look at your freewriting and make notes. Include only those parts that are relevant to your main idea.

G. Decide what background information you will need to give.

H. Organize your paragraph by chronological order.

2. Write your paragraph.

3. Revise your paragraph.
   A. Use the Revising Checklist to evaluate your paper, or ask a partner to do it.
   B. Revise your paragraph.

Revising Checklist

1. Do you tell a story or incident from a different point of view?
2. Is the point of view consistent? Do you see everything from the chosen point of view?
3. Are the events in the incident in chronological order?
4. Do you have a clear topic sentence and controlling idea?
5. Do all of the sentences support the controlling idea?
6. Do you use key words and sentence connectors to show time relationships?
7. Is the paragraph interesting and imaginative?

More Reading and Writing

Reading

The Great Surprise
by Mary Kay Mackin

This essay was written by Mary Kay Mackin, who teaches ESL at the University of New Orleans.

I will never forget the time I surprised everyone, even myself. When I was a sophomore in college in St. Paul, Minnesota, I was a member of the speech/debate team. My area of performance was oral interpretation, a category in which each contestant would memorize several short pieces of literature and deliver them with appropriate intonation and emotion in front of two or three judges. The person who gave the best interpretation won. One time our team, which consisted of about ten people, decided to participate in a city-wide contest. Each person on the team prepared his or her specialty; I chose two poems and memorized them. Another girl on our team, Barbara, entered the same category, memorizing a part of a short story. Everyone on our team, including me and the coach, thought that Barbara had the best chance of winning first place. She impressed everyone as more experienced, more **sophisticated,°** more capable than I. Everyone thought that placing second or third was the best I could hope for. I vividly remember the day of the contest, which was held at a university across town. When my scheduled time came, I went into the assigned room and delivered my poems in front of the judges. Even though I was nervous, I did my best. The judges, of course, gave no hint about what they thought, so I left the room really worried. After all the contestants had finished, we went into a large auditorium to find out the results. Our team sat together, all of us nervous and excited. When the judges announced the winners for oral interpretation, everyone on the team gasped. I had won first place and Barbara had not placed at all! **In a daze,°** I went down to the stage, accepted the trophy, and went back to my seat. I felt excited and happy but also a little embarrassed because I didn't know what I was going to say to Barbara. In the car on the way back to the campus, everyone was quiet; nobody knew what to say. At one point, I turned to Barbara to say something, but she cut me off and looked out the window at the snowy street. We never talked about the incident.

Even though I was sorry for the **awkwardness°** between Barbara and me, I was proud of myself for winning. It gave me confidence in myself and motivated me to work harder. I also learned a valuable lesson from this incident. It taught me not to depend so much on other people's assessment of myself or others, that sometimes the people who seem unlikely to do something can and will do it. We can surprise everyone, even ourselves.

cultured, aware of the world

confused, dreaming

uncomfortable feeling

Comprehension. Answer the following questions.

1. Where did this incident take place?
2. Who were the people involved?
3. What happened in this incident?
4. How did the writer feel about it?
5. What effect did this incident have on the writer's life?
6. Write five or six sentences telling the story to someone who has not read it. Tell the story in your own words.

Discussion. Discuss these questions with your classmates or teacher.

1. After winning the contest, the writer found herself in an awkward situation with Barbara. What did she do? Did she do the right thing?

2. Imagine yourself in her situation. What would you do?
3. Was the writer able to reflect on and learn from this incident?
4. Have you ever done something that surprised everyone? Tell about the incident.

Reading

From Wings of the Morning
by Orestes Lorenzo

This reading was written by Orestes Lorenzo, who was born in Cuba in 1956.

When he was a young man, Lorenzo believed in communism. He trained as a fighter pilot and became a major in the Cuban air force. As he grew older, he became disillusioned with communism and decided to escape to the United States. In December 1992, he flew a MiG-23 from Santa Clara, Cuba, to a naval air station near Key West, Florida. In the following paragraphs, Lorenzo describes the events that happened just after he landed his plane at the naval air base.

I felt my legs trembling. I couldn't figure out the stillness around me. Eventually, a light truck with a yellow blinking light above the **cab**° pulled up in front of the aircraft, signaling me to follow. Slowly, I managed to **taxi**° behind him, crossing the length of the airfield under a bright sun: the driver and his truck, me and my MiG-23, as if we were all that was left on earth. When we reached a small ramp at the far end of the field, the driver got out of his truck, indicating that I should **cut the engine.**° Seconds later, after the **shrill drone**° of the turbine had ceased, a red automobile drove up to my plane. At the wheel was an officer who turned out to be the base commander, accompanied by a sergeant who seemed to be **Hispanic.**° Both stepped out of the car as soon as they saw the MiG's **canopy**° slide open, revealing the frightened face of a Cuban pilot unable to conceal his emotion.

I took off my **helmet,**° dropped it into the **cockpit,**° and sprang onto the pavement, presenting myself at military attention to the senior officer. Then I proceeded to declare in Spanish with a trembling voice, "Mi nombre es Orestes Lorenzo."

"His name is Orestes Lorenzo."

"Soy mayor de la Fuerza Aérea Cubana . . ."

"He says he's a major in the Cuban air force."

Glossary (margin notes):

part of a truck where people sit

(verb) drive an airplane on the ground

turn off the engine

steady loud noise

Spanish-speaking

top part; roof

protective head covering

place where airplane pilot sits

". . . y pido protección a las autoridades de este país . . ."

"He's asking for protection by the authorities."

". . . por razones políticas."

"Political asylum."

high-level officer
low-level officer

The **colonel**° kept nodding to the **sergeant**° as he listened; then he fixed his eyes on me. Suddenly he broke into a smile, stepped forward, and extended a hand, saying, "Welcome to the United States."

Comprehension. Answer the following questions.

1. How did Lorenzo feel during this incident? What makes you think so? Find words and phrases in the reading to show how he felt.
2. Why was the sergeant accompanying the senior officer?
3. How did Lorenzo act toward the senior officer?
4. How did the colonel act while Lorenzo was asking for political asylum? What might the colonel have been thinking?
5. What was the colonel's final decision? How did he show it?

Reading Notes

After he arrived in the United States, Lorenzo tried for two years to get permission from the Cuban government for his wife and two children to leave Cuba. But the government would not grant permission. Then, Lorenzo made a daring rescue. He successfully flew a small old airplane to a beach near Havana, Cuba. He landed on a road and picked up his wife and children, who had secretly been told to wait for him there. Today, he and his family live in Miami, Florida.

Discussion. Discuss the following questions with your classmates or teacher.

1. How would you describe Lorenzo and what he did?
2. Have you ever done something dangerous or frightening? Tell the incident and how you felt about it.
3. Do you know anyone who has escaped from a place? Tell that person's story.

Topics for Discussion and Writing

Your teacher may ask you to discuss or write about one of the following topics.

1. Your memory of a significant historical, political, or social event, such as the celebration of the millennium, the change of political parties in Mexico, or the devastation caused by the hurricanes in Central America or the earthquake in India
2. An early memory of one of your parents
3. An event that changed your life
4. A reunion with a long-lost friend or relative

Chapter **3** Describing

Theme

Important Places

Goals

Writing

To write a paragraph describing a place

To write a topic sentence with a focused dominant impression

To support the dominant impression with descriptive details

To organize the paragraph with spatial arrangement

To improve cohesion by using connecting words for description

Reading

To read about and reflect on other writers' special places

Grammar

To review past tenses for past description and simple present tense for present description

To review sentence structures for location

To review subject/verb agreement

Getting Started

Journal Writing: An Important Place

Think about a place in your past that was important or special to you. In your journal, write about this special place. Answer the following questions:

1. What was the place?
2. What did it look like?
3. What was in the place?
4. How were things arranged?
5. How did this place make you feel?
6. Why was this place important to you?

Discussion. Describe your place to your classmates or teacher.

CNN® Video Activity: Martha's Vineyard

 One popular vacation place in the United States is Cape Cod, an area in southeastern Massachusetts. This video describes two islands off Cape Cod that are well-known for their history as well as their beauty.

Before you watch the video, discuss these questions and terms with your classmates or teacher.

1. Look at the map in Appendix A, pages 202–203. Find the United States and locate the state of Massachusetts and its islands.
2. What are some of the characteristics of the geography and history of that area?
3. The video discusses cottages on the islands. What are some ways that cottages are different from houses?
4. Study these terms: picturesque   whaling   resort

Understanding the Video

Comprehension. As you watch the video, listen for each fact written below. Decide which island it refers to. Then put a check under either "Martha's Vineyard" or "Nantucket." The first one is done as an example. After you watch the video, answer the questions.

Fact

Fact	Martha's Vineyard	Nantucket
Where the movie *Jaws* was filmed	✓	
Located seven miles off the Massachusetts coast		
Once the "Whaling Capital of the World"		
First African-American resort (Oak Bluffs)		
Old mill that still grinds corn		
Rose-covered cottages in Sconset		
Oldest working carousel		
Where red clothing is popular		
"Little Gray Lady in the Sea"		
Lighthouses and cliffs at Gay Head		

Discussion. After you watch the video, discuss these questions with your classmates or teacher.

1. What makes Martha's Vineyard and Nantucket different from other vacation places in the United States?
2. What other places in the United States are known as living museums?
3. What kinds of places would you like to visit on vacation?

Reading

Discuss this question with your classmates or teacher.

1. Look at the map in Appendix A, pages 202–203. Find Europe and draw in the Czech Republic. What do you know about this country?

Reading

Our Cottage
by Renata Strakova

This essay was written by Renata Strakova, who is studying Human Performance and Health Promotion at the University of New Orleans. She is also on the track team. She wrote this essay when she was a student in an ESL class.

When I was small, I used to go with my parents and older brother to our cottage every weekend. I spent most of my weekends and vacations there, and I developed a strong feeling for this place and its location. Our

a kind of
evergreen tree

cottage was about fifteen minutes from the nearest village. About one hundred meters below the cottage there was a tall forest of dark green **spruce**° trees. On the left side there was a hill with two meadows that were separated by a thin line of trees. On the right side were fields that had different crops every year, like potatoes or wheat. I loved these natural surroundings. The forest, meadows, and fields made a peaceful and

beautiful view

harmonious panorama.° I not only liked nature there; I also liked the house. Specifically, I liked the living room on the first floor because it was the place where my family was together most of the time. My family is very important to me and I cannot see the room without my family

nostalgic

inside. I miss it for **sentimental**° reasons.

In the room were a wooden sofa with dark red cushions, a coffee table, and three armchairs. These things had been in our house before my parents brought them to the cottage. They were old and worn, but comfortable. There was a worn red carpet on the floor that was almost the same color as the sofa. In the corner was a small table with an old black and white TV. We didn't use it very often when we were at the cottage, but it was nice to have it there. It also had come from our house. On the left wall there was an old wooden cupboard. The top part had glass doors. Inside on the shelves were antiques and souvenirs from our family. The bottom part had wooden doors, and we kept

foot-powered

clothes in it. Next to the cupboard there was an antique **treadle**° sewing machine. It had been my grandmother's. It didn't work, but it was a nice decoration in the room and it was a part of our family's history. Opposite to the cupboard there was a brick fireplace. I like to remember the times our family spent in this room, especially in the winter when we used to sit together in front of the fire and talk and listen to the sounds of the wind whistling outside.

household items
passed from older
people to their
children and
grandchildren

The room was spacious and light. It had many antique **heirlooms**° and decorations. The walls were white and covered with old pictures of landscapes and old cottages. I loved them because many of them had been in our grandparent's house. One of them, the one above the sofa, was a picture of our cottage. My parents had asked an artist to paint it. It looked exactly like the cottage. An arrangement of dried corn sat on top of the cupboard. It had been there for many years. The cupboard held many of our family's heirlooms. Most of them were from my grandparents and great-grandparents. I especially remember a dark metal can-

complicated,
heavily decorated

delabra that held three candles. It was very **intricate**° and fancy. There were also an old brown pottery vase, some ceramic mugs, and old dishes.

There was one other thing that I liked in this room. It was a large glass door in the wall opposite to the entrance door. From the glass door, there

area with table
and chairs beside a
house

was a very nice view of the grass **terrace,**° and you could go there directly from the living room. At the end of the terrace opposite to the glass door, my mother had a rock garden with many different types and colors of flowers planted around some pretty rocks. The terrace had a beautiful green **lawn.**° It was always trimmed and neat because my father mowed it every week. In the summer, we always had a table and a garden umbrella on the terrace and ate our lunch there. We enjoyed being together and looking at the peaceful scene.

area covered with grass

I liked the time spent in our cottage. I remember how my father worked hard to build this cottage. I cannot forget all the energy that my parents spent in fixing it up. That is why all of us considered the cottage our special place. It was a part of our lives.

Comprehension. Answer the following questions.

1. Where is the cottage located?
2. What surrounds the cottage?
3. What furniture is in the living room? How is it arranged?
4. What heirlooms and decorations are in the living room? Where are they?
5. Name two places where the writer's family used to sit.
6. Why did the writer like this place?
7. How did it make her feel?

Discussion. Discuss these questions with your classmates or teacher.

1. What part of the writer's description do you like the best? Why?
2. Does the description of this cottage remind you of a place that is special for your family? If so, describe the place you remember. If not, describe another place you used to visit.

NOTE: If you want to read another description of a place, read Jung Chang's description of her middle school in China on pages 68–69.

Preparing to Write

Writing about a Place in the Past

Focusing on a Dominant Impression

To describe is to tell what something looks like. When a writer describes a place, the writer tries to create a picture in words, so that the reader can see the place.

A writer must look carefully and closely at something to describe it accurately. This ability to observe and describe precisely is important in academic writing and in professional writing.

In descriptive writing, the main idea is often a **dominant impression.** A dominant impression is the main effect or impression the place has on the writer. The writer focuses on that impression and tries to communicate it to the reader. In "Our Cottage," the writer is sentimental about this place because it reminds her of her family and the times they spent there. She tries to show how special the cottage was to her and her family.

ACTIVITY 3-1   Following are some places that you have known.

1. your old bedroom
2. the kitchen of your childhood house
3. your first classroom
4. a park you used to visit

Choose one of the places listed above and do the following.

1. Freewrite about the place (see Appendix B, page 206).
2. Read your freewriting.
3. What is your dominant impression of the place? Write it here: _____

_____

The topic sentence for a descriptive paragraph should give the topic (the place you are describing) and the controlling idea (the dominant impression, idea, or attitude). It should be narrowly focused and it should be inviting to the reader. Look at the topic sentences below. Which one is more focused and interesting?

Our kitchen was a comfortable place.
The old oak table in our kitchen was the center of our family life.

ACTIVITY 3-2   Look at the dominant impression you wrote in Activity 3-1. Use the dominant impression as a controlling idea and write a focused and interesting topic sentence. Write it here: _____

_____

_____

Supporting with Descriptive Details

In descriptive writing, the writer supports the dominant impression with **descriptive details.** Descriptive details are **concrete** and **specific.** They are words that appeal to one of our five senses—sight, smell, touch, taste, or hearing.

USING SPECIFIC DETAILS

GENERAL	SPECIFIC
The chair in my bedroom was comfortable.	The worn green chair fit my body exactly.
The lake was pretty.	The turquoise lake shimmered in the morning sunlight.
The flowers smelled wonderful.	The creamy white gardenias gave off a heavy perfume.
It was windy.	The wind howled around the corner of the house.
The park benches were rough.	The old concrete park benches scraped the skin off my legs.

ACTIVITY 3-3   Read the following sentences. Underline the concrete details and tell which senses they appeal to.

1. About one hundred meters below the cottage, there was a tall forest of dark green spruce trees.
2. On the left side, there was a hill with two meadows that were separated by a thin line of trees.
3. On the left wall, there was an old wooden cupboard. The top part had glass doors. The bottom part had wooden doors.
4. I like to remember the times our family spent in this room, especially in the winter when we used to sit together in front of the fire and talk and listen to the sounds of the wind whistling outside.
5. The terrace had a beautiful green lawn. It was always trimmed and neat because my father mowed it every week.
6. The cracked concrete birdbath in our backyard, which tilted slightly to the left, was usually filled with old rainwater, soggy oak leaves, and green moss.
7. Little brown sparrows used to dart out of the bushes, turn their heads quickly from side to side, and take a few sips of the murky water.
8. A raucous blue jay would dive down out of the oak tree, screeching at the sparrows, which would flitter away with little squawks.

ACTIVITY 3-4   Use the topic sentence you wrote in Activity 3-2 and do the following.

1. Make a list of details with sense appeal to support that topic sentence.

   _____

   _____

   _____

   _____

   _____

2. Write complete sentences to support your topic sentence, using the details in your list.

   A. _____

   B. _____

   C. _____

   D. _____

Descriptive details should support the dominant impression. If you have details that do not support your dominant impression, you can do the following:

1. change your dominant impression (controlling idea)
2. take out the irrelevant details

ACTIVITY 3-5   Read the paragraph below and answer the questions that follow.

My family used to spend two months every summer at a cabin in the mountains of Colorado. To me, the most pleasant spot at the cabin was the patio. The patio was small, but I liked to sit there and enjoy the view of the mountains. Both to the left and right, there were cliffs that rose for hundreds of feet, almost straight up. There was also a steep mountain to our rear, so that the cabin was enclosed on three sides by mountains. To the front, as I sat on the patio, I could see for miles down the lovely valley between the two side mountains. The weather was usually cool, and I enjoyed feeling the mountain breezes and smelling the scent of the spruce trees. Hummingbirds would fly in and drink nectar from the flowers around the patio. Chipmunks and raccoons would occasionally come up to the patio, looking for food (we never fed them, but they were cute to look at). The only problem was the insects. Flies and small bees and gnats would start buzzing around my head almost as soon as I sat down. No matter how much I tried to swat them away, they would keep coming back. There were also some disgusting bugs called "box-elder bugs" that crawled all over the patio and chairs, and there were many ants too. Finally I would get so irritated with the bugs that I would just go back inside the cabin. They almost ruined the patio for me.

1. What is the controlling idea of the paragraph?
2. Do all of the details support the controlling idea?
3. Suggest ways that the writer could revise the paragraph.
4. Below is the writer's revision of the paragraph. She has added the parts in bold print and deleted the parts crossed out. Read the revision and answer the questions that follow.

> My family used to spend two months every summer at a **log** cabin in the mountains of Colorado. To me, the most pleasant spot at the cabin was the patio. The patio, **which was made of plain grey cement,** was small, **about 9 by 12 feet,** but I liked to sit there **in a worn wooden lawn chair** and enjoy the view of the mountains. Both to the left and right, there were **huge red rock** cliffs that rose for hundreds of feet, almost straight up. There was also a steep **spruce-covered** mountain to our rear, so that the cabin was enclosed on three sides by mountains. **With mountains almost all around, I felt protected and comfortable.** To the front, as I sat on the patio, I could see for miles down the lovely **green** valley between the two side mountains. **In the valley were a series of ponds that shimmered and sparkled in the sunlight. In the distance was a mountain that looked like it was covered with green velvet. What a sight!** The weather was usually cool, and I enjoyed feeling the mountain breezes and smelling the scent of the spruce trees. **Shimmering green** hummingbirds **with red spots** would fly in and drink nectar from the **white and red petunias** around the patio. **Tiny** chipmunks and **fat** raccoons would occasionally come up to the patio, **sit on their hind legs, and beg** for food. ~~(We never fed them, but they were cute to look at.)~~ **I could spend hours sitting on the patio, sometimes reading a book, but more often just drinking in the atmosphere.** ~~The only problem was the insects. Flies and small bees and gnats would start buzzing around my head almost as soon as I sat down. No matter how much I tried to swat them away, they would keep coming back. There were also some disgusting bugs called "box-elder bugs" that crawled all over the patio and chairs, and there were many ants too. Finally I would get so irritated with the bugs that I would just go back inside the cabin. They almost ruined the patio for me.~~

5. Did the writer change the controlling idea of the paragraph?
6. Why did the writer delete the parts crossed out?
7. Why did the writer add the parts in bold print?
8. What parts did the writer add? Why did she add those parts?

Organizing by Spatial Arrangement

In descriptive writing it is often important for the readers to be able to "see" in their minds the place being described. To help the readers see the place, the writer must organize the supporting details according to a logical arrangement. Often, in descriptive writing, this arrangement is spatial. In **spatial organization,** the writer first describes one part of the place, then moves on to describe another part of the place, and so on. The writer thus shows the relationship of things to each other in space and guides the reader through space.

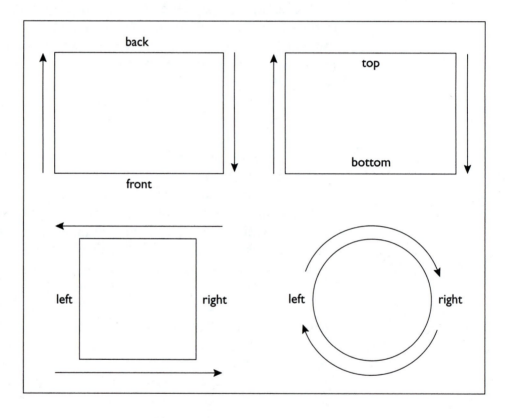

ACTIVITY 3-6   Look at the revised paragraph in Activity 3-5 and tell how it is organized.

ACTIVITY 3-7   Read the paragraph below and answer the questions that follow.

When I was in Mexico, my family used to visit my grandmother every two weeks. Most of the time, she was in the kitchen. I enjoyed her kitchen because it was a warm, familiar place. To get into the kitchen, we had to bend down a little because the door was short. As soon as we got in, my grandmother, with a happy smile, offered us chairs and began asking questions. When we were talking to her, I enjoyed looking around her kitchen, which had the appearance of an old, traditional Mexican house. It was all made with natural resources. The floor was made of packed earth and the roof was made of woven palms. The walls were interlaced poles that let the light through. In the corner on the left side of the door was the fireplace where she used to cook, always using firewood. She also had a cabinet adjacent to the fireplace, where she kept her kitchen utensils. Near the cabinet was a small table where she washed dishes. On the right side of the door she had another table and beside it was another cabinet where she put her groceries. These furnishings were always tidy and they were always the same. Almost in the middle of the kitchen by the right side was the dinner table; this table was bigger than the others, having six chairs. The table and chairs were very old and pretty; they were made of wood and the chair seats were of woven palm leaf. We spent many hours at this table eating traditional food and talking to my grandmother. I always enjoyed the time I spent in her kitchen, talking, eating, and looking at the warm, familiar place she had.

—Victor Amaya

1. Underline the topic sentence of the paragraph.
2. Circle the controlling idea.
3. Underline the details that support the controlling idea.
4. For each detail, tell which sense it appeals to.
5. The writer uses spatial organization. How does he begin the spatial description?
6. After he is seated in the kitchen, what does he describe next?
7. What objects does he use to show the location of the fireplace, cabinets, and small tables (*to the right of . . . , to the left of . . .*)?
8. What are the last objects he describes? Where are they?
9. Where do you think the writer is sitting as he looks at the room?

Sometimes in descriptive writing the writer uses order of importance to organize the paragraph. In this case the writer will begin with the most important item, which is often something outstanding or unusual, and then go on to describe the less important items.

ACTIVITY 3-8 Look at the topic sentence and support you wrote in Activity 3-4. Decide how you would organize these into a paragraph. Then write the paragraph.

Writing

Writing Assignment 1: Descriptive

Now you are going to write a paragraph describing a place.

1. PREPARE TO WRITE.

    A. First, think about a place you would like to describe. You may choose one of the topics listed below.

    A Private Place

    > A room in your childhood house
    >
    > A room in your first apartment
    >
    > The yard or patio of your old house
    >
    > The view from the balcony of your first apartment
    >
    > A special place where you played as a child

    A Public Place

    > Your old classroom
    >
    > The office where you once worked
    >
    > A room in the building where you once worked
    >
    > A park you used to visit
    >
    > A church or temple you used to attend
    >
    > A market you used to go to

    B. Get ideas about your place by drawing a sketch and freewriting about it (see Appendix B, pages 204–208, for an explanation and example of these methods).

    C. Decide on a controlling idea and write an interesting topic sentence.

    D. Choose descriptive details to support your controlling idea.

    E. Organize your support by spatial arrangement or order of importance.

2. WRITE THE PARAGRAPH.

    Remember your audience. Your readers do not know what your place looks like, so you must paint a picture with words.

3. REVISE THE PARAGRAPH.

A. Ask a partner to evaluate your paragraph using the Paragraph Guidelines, or do it yourself using the Revising Checklist.

B. Revise your paragraph.

Paragraph Guidelines

1. Write out the topic sentence and circle the controlling idea.
2. List the details the writer uses.
3. Does the writer have a clear topic sentence and controlling idea?
4. Are the details descriptive? Do they appeal to your senses?
5. Do all of the details support the controlling idea?
6. What details do you especially like?
7. What kind of organization does the writer use?
8. What part of the paragraph did you enjoy the most?
9. What part would you like to know more about?

Revising Checklist

1. Do you describe a place?
2. Do you have a clear topic sentence and controlling idea?
3. Do you use sensory details to support the topic sentence?
4. Do all of the details support the controlling idea?
5. Do you organize the paragraph by spatial arrangement or order of importance?
6. Is the paragraph interesting?

Using Language Effectively

Cohesion: Connecting Words for Description

In writing description, the writer needs to show the relationship of things in space. Spatial relationships are often shown with key words that are prepositional phrases telling **where.**

WORDS TO INDICATE SPATIAL RELATIONSHIPS

KEY WORDS

above	facing	on
across	from	on either side (of)

against		on top (of)
along	in	outside
around	inside	over
at	in front (of)	
	in the middle (of)	separated by
behind	inside	supported by
below		surrounded by
beneath	next to	surrounding
beside		to the left (of)
between		to the right (of)
		under

Examples

About one hundred meters below the cottage, there was a tall forest of dark green spruce trees.

On the left side, there was a hill with two meadows that were separated **by a thin line of trees.**

Both to the left and right, there were cliffs that rose **for hundreds of feet.**

ACTIVITY 3-9   Read the following paragraph. Underline all of the prepositional phrases that show location or direction.

My old classroom was interesting because three sides of the classroom were made of glass. I enjoyed sitting close to the windows and looking at the view. On the left-hand side of the class, I could easily see the football field. In the mornings, it was full of students exercising. There was an army camp in front of the playing ground not far away from the school. It was fabulous to see the soldiers marching up and down the field. Farther in the distance, I had the advantage of seeing the city of Nicosia. It was enjoyable to see the houses, the buildings, the hospital, and the river close to it. The view from the back of the classroom was also panoramic. Close to the school there was a beautiful park with many trees around it. Not far from the park was a hippodrome for horse racing. Since I like horses, I was interested to see the horses running in the hippodrome. Farther in the distance, I could enjoy the view of the snowy mountains. On the right side of the class was the road. I was always interested to see the drivers in a hurry in the morning. Behind the road was a thick forest, which was appealing during the winter. The position of the classroom with its panoramic view made me feel like

I was dreaming. Although I was only a child when I studied in that classroom, I will never forget it.

—*Andreas Andreou*

ACTIVITY 3-10   Find a picture of a place in a magazine. Bring it to class. With a partner, explain the location of the items in the picture.

Grammar Review

The following grammar points will help you write description. If you want to review them, turn to the pages listed below.

Verb Tenses	Page 228
Past Tense for Past Description	Page 228
Simple Present Tense for Present Description	Page 228
Sentence Structure for Location	Page 230
There + Be	Page 230
Adverb/Verb/Subject	Page 232
Subject-Verb Agreement	Page 232

Using the Internet

INTERNET ACTIVITY   Many Web sites use pictures to give information or add interest. Choose one of the places listed below. Use a search engine such as Google, Yahoo!, or Excite to find a picture of a place.

1. Go to a museum's Web site and find a picture of a painting that you like.
2. Imagine that you are going to take a trip to your favorite city and you need to find a hotel. Go to a Web site that lists hotels in that city and find a hotel that shows pictures of its rooms. Choose the room you want to stay in.
3. Imagine that you are going to take a trip to a place you have never visited before. You want to see what the place looks like. Find a picture of the place. (Choose a specific place like Mount Fuji, Glacier Lake, the Pyramid of the Sun, the Great Wall of China.)

Now do the following.

1. Without showing the picture to a partner, describe the place. As you describe it, ask your partner to draw the place on a piece of paper. In your description, use connecting words to indicate spatial relationships, the simple

present tense, sentence structures for location, and correct subject/verb agreement.

2. When you have finished describing the picture, compare it with your partner's drawing. How well did you describe the place?

3. Your teacher may ask you to write a paragraph describing the picture.

Preparing to Write

Writing about a Place in the Present

In the previous assignment, you wrote about a place you remembered from your past. A writer can also describe a place he or she is currently familiar with. For example, a writer might describe a favorite room or view.

ACTIVITY 3-11   Read the paragraph below and answer the questions that follow.

The first thing we did as soon as we came to the U.S.A. about two years ago was to search for an apartment in order not to live with one of our relatives. After looking for one month to find a suitable apartment, I finally found the apartment where we have been living. It includes a living room, three bedrooms, and a kitchen. Probably the living room is my favorite room of all because we often gather together after we come home from work or school. It is a comfortable room for our family. Entering the living room from the front door, we can see a new piano in the corner, with a vase of colorful flowers on it. In the opposite corner stands a Sony television, which I bought for my children to watch cartoons and for us to see films and get the daily news. There is a sofa next to the piano, a loveseat beside the TV, and also a low table between them. This is a comfortable place to sit while we watch TV or talk. On one of the light blue walls is a tranquil picture of the sea. The floor is covered with a dark red carpet, which my children like to play on. They also like to sit on it when they watch TV. The large window is shaded by a light colored curtain, giving the room a soft, bright feeling. A ceiling fan with small lights is hanging from the ceiling; whenever the fan and lights are on, we can see dangling images, which are reflected from the furniture in the room. Generally, our living room is a place where we receive our guests, gather together to discuss any topic, and enjoy our leisure time.

—*Bachvan Doan*

1. Write out the topic sentence and circle the controlling idea.
2. Make a list of details the writer uses to support her dominant impression.

Writing

Writing Assignment 2: Descriptive

For this assignment, you are going to write a paragraph describing a place you are familiar with now.

1. PREPARE TO WRITE.

    A. Choose a place that you want to write about. You may choose one of the topics listed below.

    A room in your current house

    Your dormitory room

    The view from your balcony

    This classroom

    A place in the library where you often study

    Another place on campus

    A park you often go to

    B. Get ideas about your place by using one of the methods given in Appendix B.

    C. Decide on a controlling idea and write an interesting topic sentence.

    D. Choose descriptive details to support your controlling idea.

    E. Organize your support by spatial arrangement or order of importance.

2. WRITE THE PARAGRAPH.

3. REVISE THE PARAGRAPH.

    A. Use the Revising Checklist to evaluate your paragraph, or ask a partner to do it.

    B. Revise your paragraph.

Revising Checklist

1. Do you have a topic sentence that focuses on your dominant impression of the place?
2. Do all of the ideas in the paragraph support the dominant impression?
3. Do you have enough support, or do you need to add more?

4. Is your support descriptive and detailed? Do the details paint a picture for the reader?
5. Have you used spatial organization or some other logical method?
6. Have you used appropriate connecting words?
7. Have you used appropriate verb tenses?
8. Is the paragraph interesting?

More Reading and Writing

Reading

From Wild Swans: Three Daughters of China
by Jung Chang

In this reading, Jung Chang describes the middle school she attended in Sichuan province, China, in 1964, when she was twelve years old. Today Jung Chang teaches at London University.

I loved the school from the moment I walked in. It had an imposing gate with a broad roof of blue tiles and carved **eaves.**° A flight of stone stairs led up to it, and the loggia was supported by six red-timber columns. Symmetrical rows of dark-green cypresses **enhanced**° the atmosphere of solemnity leading into the interior.

The school had been founded in 141 B.C. It was the first school set up by a local government in China. At its center was a magnificent temple, formerly dedicated to **Confucius.**° It was well preserved, but was not functioning as a temple any longer. Inside were half a dozen ping-pong tables, separated by the massive columns. In front of the carved doors, down a long flight of stairs, lay **extensive**° grounds designed to provide a majestic approach to the temple. A two-story teaching **block**° had been erected, which cut off the grounds from a brook crossed by three little arched bridges, with sculptures of miniature lions and other animals sitting on their sandstone edges. Beyond the bridges was a beautiful garden surrounded by peach and plane trees. Two giant bronze **incense**° burners were set at the bottom of the stairs in front of the temple, although there was no longer any blue smoke curling up and lingering in the air above them. The grounds on the sides of the temple had been converted into basketball and volleyball courts. Farther along were two lawns where we used to sit or lie in spring and enjoy the sun during lunch breaks. Behind the temple was another lawn, beyond which lay a big orchard at the foot of a small hill covered with trees, vines, and herbs.

Margin glosses:
edges of a roof

added to

Chinese teacher and philosopher who lived in 500 B.C..

very large building

something that is burned to give a pleasant smell

located here and
there

Dotted around° were laboratories where we studied biology and chemistry, learned to use microscopes, and dissected dead animals. In the lecture theaters, we watched teaching films. For after-school activities, I joined the biology group which strolled around the hill and the back garden with the teacher learning the names and characteristics of the different plants. There were temperature-controlled breeding cases for us to observe how tadpoles and ducklings broke out of their eggs. In the spring, the school was a sea of pink because of all the peach trees. But what I liked most was the two-story library, built in the traditional Chinese style. The building was encircled on both floors by loggias, and the outside of these was enclosed by a row of gorgeously painted seats which were shaped like wings. I had a favorite corner in these "wing seats" (fei-lai-yi) where I used to sit for hours reading, occasionally stretching my arm out to touch the fan-shaped leaves of a rare gingko tree. There was a pair of them outside the front gate of the library, towering and elegant. They were the only sight that could **distract me**° from my books.

take my thoughts
away from

Comprehension. Answer these questions.

1. Describe the gate.
2. What building is at the center of the school?
3. What is the temple used for?
4. What other buildings are on the school grounds?
5. What are some of the activities Chang participated in?
6. Where was Chang's favorite place? What did she do there?
7. How does Chang feel about this place? How do you know?

Discussion. Discuss the following questions with your classmates or teacher.

1. What kind of a person do you think Chang is? Why?
2. What part of the reading do you especially like? Why?
3. Do you have mostly happy or unhappy memories of your middle school? Why?

Topics for Discussion and Writing

Your teacher may ask you to discuss or write about one or more of the following topics.

1. A famous place in your country that does not exist any more
2. A place you visited that you had negative feelings about
3. A place you visited recently in this country
4. A mysterious place
5. Your favorite movie theater

Chapter **4** Analyzing Reasons (Causes)

Theme

People and Their Behavior

Goals

Writing

To write a paragraph analyzing reasons

To support the main idea with factual details and examples

To distinguish between generalizations and support

To organize by points

To improve cohesion by using connecting words for examples and reasons and by using consistent pronouns

To explain subpoints

To outline a paragraph

Reading

To read about and analyze why people do what they do

Grammar

To review present perfect tense and consistency of verb tenses

To review adjective clauses

Getting Started

Journal Writing: A Person I Admire

"Why do we do what we do?" We often ask the question "why" about other people's behavior and about our own lives. Think about a person that you admire. Ask yourself why you admire him or her. In your journal, write about this person and the reasons for your admiration. Answer the following questions:

1. Who is this person?
2. What is his or her relationship to you?
3. What are some reasons you admire this person?
4. Did this person do or say something specific to gain your respect? What was it?

Discussion. Tell your classmates or teacher about the person and the reasons you admire him or her.

CNN® Video Activity: Educator Awards

Many teachers care about their students' lives, not just their schoolwork. The video concerns a music teacher who won an award for his special talents.

Before you watch the video, discuss these questions with your classmates or teacher.

1. What qualities do students want their teacher to have?
2. What qualities make a teacher excellent, not just good?
3. Why do people become teachers?

Understanding the Video

Comprehension. Read the following questions. As you watch the video, take brief notes. After you watch the video, answer the questions.

1. Why does Roy Anthony, Jr. love teaching?
2. How long has Anthony been teaching?
3. What is the Milken Award?
4. How much money is given to the winner of the Milken Award?
5. What qualities does Anthony try to teach his students?
6. How do the other teachers at his school feel about him?

Discussion. After you watch the video, discuss these questions with your classmates or teacher.

1. What is the meaning of the sign in Mr. Anthony's classroom: "Winning is not everything, but the effort to win is"?
2. Should teachers at all levels—elementary, high school, university—take an interest in their students' personal lives? Why or why not?
3. Have you ever had a teacher like Mr. Anthony? Describe him or her.
4. What advice would you give to young people who want to become teachers?

Reading

Discuss these questions with your classmates or teacher.

1. Look at the photographs below and on page 73. For each one, answer these questions:
   a. Tell as much as you can about the person.
   b. Do you admire him or her? Why or why not?
2. Fill in the empty box on page 73 with a sketch of someone you admire. Beside it, tell who the person is and why you admire him or her.

Julia Alvarez

Jackie Chan

Daw Aung San Suu Kyi   **Stephen Hawking**

My hero

Reading

From A Celebration of Teachers
by Kristin Hunter

This essay was written by Kristin Hunter, a novelist and playwright. It was published in a book of essays in which well-known people wrote about teachers whom they admired and who had influenced them.

The teacher who did the most to encourage me was, as it happens, my aunt.

She was Myrtle C. Manigault, the wife of my mother's brother Bill, when she taught me in second grade at all-black Sumner School in Camden, New Jersey. Now she is Mrs. Myrtle M. Stratton, retired and residing in Haddonfield, New Jersey.

During my childhood and youth, Aunt Myrtle encouraged me to develop every aspect of my **potential,**° without regard for what was considered practical or possible for black females. I liked to sing; she listened to my voice and pronounced it good. I couldn't dance; she taught me the basic **jitterbug**° steps. She took me to the theater—not just children's theater but adult comedies and dramas—and her faith that I could appreciate adult plays was not disappointed.

possible abilities

a dance popular in the 1940s

Aunt Myrtle also took down books from her extensive library and shared them with me. We had books at home, but they were all serious classics. Even as a child I had a strong bent towards humor, and I will never forget the joy of discovering Don Marquis's *Archy & Mehitabel* through her.

Most important, perhaps, Aunt Myrtle provided my first opportunity to write for publication. A writer herself for one of the black newspapers, the Philadelphia edition of the *Pittsburgh Courier,* she suggested my name to the editor as a "youth columnist." My column, begun at age fourteen, was supposed to cover teenage social activities—and it did—but it also gave me the **latitude**° to write on many other subjects as well as the habit of gathering material, the discipline of meeting deadlines, and, after college graduation six years later, a solid **portfolio**° of published material that carried my **byline**° and was my passport to a series of writing jobs.

freedom

collection

writer's name on a story

Today Aunt Myrtle, independently and through her organization (she is a founding member of The Links, Inc.), is still an **ardent booster**° of culture and of her "favorite niece." She reads omnivorously, attends writers' readings, persuades her clubs to support artists, and never lets me succumb to discouragement for very long. As I told her theater club

strong, enthusiastic supporter

recently, she is "as brilliant and beautiful and tough as a diamond." And, like a diamond, she has reflected a bright, multifaceted image of possibilities to every pupil who has crossed her path.

Comprehension. Answer the following questions.

1. What is the relationship between Kristin Hunter and the woman she writes about?
2. What are some ways that Myrtle Manigault encouraged Hunter?
3. Did Hunter learn to appreciate adult plays?
4. What difference was there between the kind of books Hunter had available at her home and those her aunt introduced her to?
5. What was the most important thing that Manigault did for her niece?
6. What did Hunter learn from this experience?
7. What are some of the activities the aunt does now?
8. Hunter compares her aunt to a diamond. Explain this comparison.

Discussion. Discuss this question with your classmates or teacher.

1. Tell about a teacher or older adult who encouraged you.

NOTE: If you want to read another essay analyzing reasons, read "Teenagers and Stress" by David Inman on pages 94–96.

Preparing to Write

Focusing on a Main Idea

The main idea of an essay or paragraph is usually a generalization. A **generalization** is a statement about a person, place, or idea that is considered to be true most of the time. For example, most people would consider the following statement to be generally true: People exercise in order to stay healthy.

Analyzing Reasons

To analyze is to look carefully at something in order to try to understand it. Literally, it means to divide something into its parts. For example, when chemists analyze a compound, they separate out the different elements the compound is composed of in order to know what parts make it up. Similarly, when you analyze a paragraph to find its topic sentence and support, you are dividing it into two parts.

Analysis is a common way of thinking, both in college and at work. One kind of analysis that you do frequently is to look for **causes** or **reasons** for something. When you analyze causes, you ask the question **why.** In a biology class, you might ask why bats sleep during the daytime; as a social worker, you might ask why people use drugs; in your personal life, you might ask why your roommate acted in a certain way or why you made a particular decision. If you think about one of these questions, you will probably come up with one or more reasons to explain the behavior. In this case, you have analyzed the situation, divided it into parts, and now should understand it better.

In writing, there are a number of ways to approach a topic. The writer can narrate a story, describe something, or analyze something. Looking for reasons is a common way to analyze a topic. In this approach to writing, the writer supports the main idea with reasons.

Supporting with Details

No matter what kind of approach (narrating, describing, analyzing) the writer takes to the topic, he or she must support the main idea with **details.** In narrating and describing, the writer focuses on descriptive details—those that appeal to the reader's senses. In analyzing, the writer often focuses on factual details.

Factual details are facts and information that explain the main idea and make it specific. They provide answers to the questions *who, what, why, when, where,* and *how.* Factual details make the main idea believable to the reader and thus provide effective support.

Read the following paragraph. What details could the writer add? What *who, what, why, when, where, how* questions would you like answers to? Make an *X* in the paragraph where you would like to know more details.

I have always admired my first-grade teacher. One reason I admire him is that he made learning to read easy. He had a very good method for teaching reading. First we learned the letters of the alphabet. Then we learned short words. Finally, we put the short words together into sentences.

Here are some questions you might want to know the answers to:

Who was your teacher?
Where was your school?
How did you learn the letters of the alphabet?
What short words did you learn?
How did you learn them?
What short sentences did you learn?
How did you put the words together into sentences?

Read the revised paragraph on the next page. The details the writer has added are underlined.*

---

* The writer has also added an example, which is not underlined. Examples are discussed in the next section.

I have always admired my first-grade teacher, <u>Mr. Pauls.</u> One reason I admire him is that he made learning to read easy for us <u>first graders at Pulaski Grade School.</u> He had a very good method for teaching reading. First, we learned the letters of the alphabet. <u>We did this by using flash cards that had the letters on them. Mr. Pauls held them up and we identified the letter. We also played games with them.</u> In one game, for example, he hid the flash cards around the room and each of us had to find one. We learned the letters easily this way because it was fun. Then, we learned short words <u>like "dog," "cat," "see," and "run." He had colored pictures, showing the item or activity, so it was easy to remember them. We made up stories about the pictures too.</u> Finally, we put the short words together into sentences <u>like "see the dog run."</u> These were easy to learn since we already knew the letters and words. Mr. Pauls was a good teacher because he had an effective method of teaching reading.

The added details help the reader understand the main idea better. They make the paragraph clearer and more interesting.

ACTIVITY 4-1   Read the following paragraphs. Make an *X* in the paragraphs where the audience would like more information. Then write out questions the writer should answer in the paragraph.

1.   Advertising makes my life miserable because I have to fight with my desires all the time. I want to buy something all the time. Sometimes I don't sleep if I want something. Even when I should be studying I daydream about what I want.

—Ditmar Hospital

2.   Language is one of the most difficult things foreigners face. They find it difficult to ask for directions to hospitals, hotels, etc. They also can find it difficult to buy things.

—Ali Al-Ghamdi

3.   Credit cards also have a bad side. Some people don't know how to control themselves and use their credit cards without thinking. They will be in serious trouble at the end of the month.

—Saira Rodriguez

4.   In school, I am studying English and Mathematics. I am trying very hard to succeed in my courses. If I have problems in math, I go to see the lecturer to discuss the problems. Sometimes I have trouble understanding the explanation in English. Then, I study that part again.

—Cheng Kooi Koay

Supporting with Examples

In analytical writing, the writer often uses **examples** to support a generalization. An example is a representative of a group.

Examples:	Smoking cigarettes is an example of an addictive behavior.
	Football is an example of a team sport.
	The Honda Accord is an example of a popular car.

What group does the example below represent?

> We also played games with them. In one game, for example, he hid the flash cards around the room and each of us had to find one.

In choosing examples to prove a point, the writer needs to consider how many examples to give. He or she may give several short examples or one long example. In any case, the examples need to be fair; they need to be actually representative of the group and not exceptions to the rule.

The writer needs to move down the levels of generality to include specific examples.

Level 1	General	food
Level 2	More Specific	fruits
Level 3	More Specific	apples
Level 4	Most Specific	Golden Delicious

Level 1	General	method for teaching reading
Level 2	More Specific	learned letters of alphabet
Level 3	More Specific	used flash cards
Level 4	More Specific	played games
Level 5	Most Specific	hid the flash cards/found them

ACTIVITY 4-2　Choose five of the topics below. For each one, make a list showing the levels of generality. Be as specific as you can.

Example:	Level 1	transportation
	Level 2	land vehicles
	Level 3	cars
	Level 4	Chrysler cars
	Level 5	Jeep
	Level 6	Cherokee

colleges	machines
clothes	flowers
diseases	jewelry
fast food	books
movies	buildings

Read the following paragraph. Notice that the ideas become more and more specific, moving down the levels of generality.

Aunt Myrtle also took down **books** from her extensive library and shared them with me. We had books at home, but they were all serious classics. Even as a child I had a strong bent towards **humor,** and I will never forget the joy of discovering Don Marquis's ***Archy & Mehitabel*** through her.	Level 1 General Level 2 More Specific *Level 3 Most Specific*

A diagram of the paragraph looks like this:

Aunt Myrtle shared books with me	Topic sentence introduces topic and controlling idea
I had only read classics, but I liked **humorous books**	Next two sentences narrow topic to a general example
She introduced me to *Archy & Mehitabel*	Next sentence narrows to a specific example

Notice that the paragraph introduces the topic (books), narrows to a particular kind of book (humorous books), and then gives a specific example of a humorous book. In your writing, you need to include the level of the specific example.

ACTIVITY 4-3 Following are some topic sentences. For each one, give a general example and a specific instance of that example. The first one is done as an example.

1. I admire my mother because she is patient.
    a. She doesn't scold me when I make mistakes.
    b. When she taught me to drive the car, I almost hit a tree, but she didn't get angry. She just told me calmly to back up and try again.

2. I admire _____ because _____

    _____

    a. _____

    _____

    b. _____

    _____

3. I like/do not like living away from home because_____

    _____

    a. _____

    _____

    b. _____

    _____

4. Teenagers feel stress because_____

    _____

    a. _____

    _____

    b. _____

    _____

Distinguishing between Generalization and Support

The topic sentence in an analytical paragraph should be a generalization. The support should be specific details and examples.

ACTIVITY 4-4   Read the following topics and sets of sentences. For each set, determine which sentence is a generalization and which ones are specific support.

1. Why we eat junk food
    a. Advertisers say junk food will make us happy.
    b. An ad for Fritos shows smiling people at a party gathered around a bowl of Fritos and dip.

   c. The people are discouraged before they eat the junk food but happy afterwards.

   d. The ads for Coke always have upbeat music and dancing.

2. Why I decided on this school
   a. The program covers aspects of business administration that some programs don't.
   b. It has the best program in business administration in the area.
   c. It has an entire course in marketing techniques for Asian countries.
   d. How to incorporate computers into every aspect of retailing is covered in detail.

3. Why people smoke cigarettes
   a. In the movies, the most sophisticated characters smoke.
   b. Ingrid Bergman and Humphrey Bogart in *Casablanca* are constantly lighting up.
   c. John Wayne, who plays the hero in many American westerns, smokes in *True Grit, The Treasure of the Sierra Madre,* and *The Sons of Katie Elder.*
   d. It makes them look cool.

Organizing by Points

Analytical writing is often organized according to **points.** Points are the major parts or divisions of the topic. They are the ideas the writer will write about. The writer gives two, three, or four subpoints to support the main idea. Each subpoint is further supported with details and examples.

The writer needs to decide on a logical way to order the subpoints. The writer needs to think about which point to put first, which one second, and so on, following a principle of organization. While there is no set way to order major points, some common principles of organization are as follows:

1. Order of importance—from the least important to the most important
2. Order of familiarity—from the most familiar to the least familiar
3. Order of time—from the past to the present

Look at the paragraph about Mr. Pauls on page 77. How does this writer order the main points of support?

ACTIVITY 4-5   Study the following topic sentences and points of support. Decide on a logical order for the points of support. There may be more than one logical way to order them. Be prepared to explain your ordering.

1. **One problem for the elderly is poor health.**
   a. **The worst thing is that they lose their bladder control so diligently gained during childhood. They can't prevent it even though they**

are aware of it and embarrassed about it. This seems to be a major reason why people put the elderly in nursing homes. They don't have time to take care of them and feel annoyed whenever they have to.

b. Looking at themselves in the mirror, they see many wrinkles.
c. Their failing eyesight requires bifocals or even trifocals.
d. They need a hearing aid because they are nearly deaf.

—Bachvan Doan

2. When I was attending Byron High School in Illinois three years ago, I felt at a disadvantage in communicating with people in a different language, English.

a. I had a strong accent, so when I was speaking it was very hard to make people understand what I was talking about.
b. Also, some students in the government class made fun of me because I couldn't answer some questions about American government. It was not easy to understand this subject in English.
c. I also felt different about myself. When I speak Japanese, it is easy to express myself and feel everything from my heart. Since I was speaking a different language, I couldn't feel real.
d. I also noticed that Japanese people often try to speak English for American people in Japan to show some respect. But here it was different. I had to speak English even though I couldn't. That was really tough for me.

—Chiemi Hashio

Writing

Writing Assignment 1: Analyzing Reasons

Now you are going to write a paragraph analyzing your behavior.

1. PREPARE TO WRITE.

A. First think about an aspect of yourself that you would like to analyze. It may be one of the topics listed below.

Reasons or Causes for a Decision in Your Life

Why did you make a particular decision?

Why did you choose this school?

Why did you choose your major?

Why did you choose to live in the dormitory?

Why did you break off an important friendship?

Why is _____ your hobby?

Why do you admire _____?

B. After you have decided on your topic, get ideas by using one of the methods given in Appendix B. You may want to brainstorm.

C. Decide on a controlling idea and write a topic sentence.

D. Choose effective supporting points.

E. Think of details and examples to support your points.

F. Organize your points in a logical way.

2. WRITE THE PARAGRAPH.

3. REVISE THE PARAGRAPH.

A. Ask a partner to evaluate your paper using the Paragraph Guidelines, or do it yourself using the Revising Checklist.

B. Revise your paragraph.

Paragraph Guidelines

1. Write out the generalization (topic sentence) and circle the controlling idea.
2. List the support the writer gives.
3. Does the writer have a clear, focused topic sentence and controlling idea?
4. Does the writer give enough support?
5. Does all of the support relate to the topic sentence?
6. What kind of organization does the writer use?
7. What part of the paragraph did you enjoy the most?
8. What part would you like to know more about?

Revising Checklist

1. Do you have a clear topic sentence and controlling idea?
2. Do you have enough support?
3. Does all of the support relate to the topic sentence?
4. Do you have logical organization?
5. Is the paragraph interesting?

Using Language Effectively

Cohesion: Connecting Words to Indicate Examples*

The writer may signal an example with a transitional word or with key words in a sentence.

WORDS TO INDICATE EXAMPLES

KEY WORDS	TRANSITIONAL WORDS
an example (of _____) is	for example
another example (of _____) is	for instance
the most important example (of _____) is	in particular
_____ is an example of	

Examples

An example of a hero is Nelson Mandela.

The Jeep Grand Cherokee is an example of a popular SUV.

Examples

We also played games with them. In one game, **for example,** he hid the flash cards around the room and each of us had to find one.

WORDS TO INDICATE THE SEQUENCE OF EXAMPLES OR POINTS

TRANSITIONAL WORDS
first
second
next
then
last
finally

Example

First, we learned the letters of the alphabet.

* You may want to review the four kinds of connecting words presented in Chapter 1, pages 18–20.

WORDS TO ADD INFORMATION

TRANSITIONAL WORDS

also

moreover

in addition

Example

Also, some students in the government class
made fun of me.

Cohesion: Connecting Words to Indicate Reasons or Causes

The writer may signal reasons or causes in two ways.

WORDS TO INDICATE REASONS OR CAUSES

KEY WORDS	SUBORDINATORS
because of	because
one reason (_____) is	since
another reason (_____) is	
Examples	*Examples*
Because of the differences in language, I couldn't feel real.	Advertising makes my life miserable **because** I have to fight with my desires all the time.
One reason I admire Mr. Pauls is his method for teaching reading.	**Since I** was speaking in a different language, I couldn't feel real.

ACTIVITY 4-6   Add appropriate connecting words to the paragraph below. Use the grammar and punctuation of the sentences to help you choose the right answers.

_____ I chose to live in an apartment and not to live in the dormitory is that I like my privacy. At home, I always had my own room and I enjoyed being in my room by myself. I guess I feel that my room is my own little universe and I can do whatever I want there. _____, if I want to listen to music and dance, I can. No one is there to look at me. _____, being alone allows me to study in my own way. When I study, I need everything to be quiet. If someone is talking or playing the radio, it bothers me. When I was living at home, my younger sister used to come into my room and want to look at my things and talk while I was studying. I found I couldn't study when she was there because it was so distracting. I learned then that privacy is important to me and that living in the dormitory wouldn't work for me.

ACTIVITY 4-7 The following paragraph does not have connecting words. Underline the sentences that should contain connecting words. Rewrite the paragraph, adding appropriate connecting words to those sentences.

People lie to be recognized by others. We expect others to have a certain response toward us. People want to have good reputations, reach a high position, and be promoted. Maybe we may have a job that does not give us an opportunity to show off, so we may prefer to tell lies in order to be accepted by others. A man who is a messenger in a bank presents himself as the vice-president of the bank. A football player who doesn't get into the game very much tells his friends he is the star of the team. People tell lies to avoid a person or situation. You may want to avoid a person but you do not want to show that directly, so you must find a believable excuse. A classmate asks you to study with him, but you tell him you have plans to go out with your girlfriend.

—*Andreas Andreou*

Cohesion: Pronoun Consistency

Pronouns must agree, or be consistent, with the noun they refer to. Look at these sentences:

Students don't go to class because **their** parents don't force **them** to.
Students don't go to class because **his** parents don't force **him** to.

In the first sentence, the pronouns *their* and *them* agree with the plural noun *students*. In the second sentence, *his* and *him* do not agree with the plural noun *students*.

ACTIVITY 4-8   Each of the following sentences has errors in pronoun consistency. Correct the errors in pronoun agreement. Write the correct words above the line. The first one is done as an example.

1. If we want to take advantage of our education, ~~you~~ *we* should study every day.

2. A lot of students have a difficult time when they go to college and you have a roommate.

3. Because they are away from parents and are living with other people, you have to make decisions by yourself.

4. I have heard that freshman girls gain fifteen pounds during their first year. It is because they are not forced to go to class by her parent.

5. Also, the student tries a lot of things behind their parents' back.

6. It is fun for a student to be on their own, but they have more responsibility for himself.

7. Each person has to find out who you are and what he wants in his life.

8. A lot of people give a student this advice when you have been feeling depressed or when they don't know what to do about a girlfriend or boyfriend.

ACTIVITY 4-9   The following paragraph has errors in pronoun consistency. Correct the errors in pronoun agreement. Write the correct words above the line.

I enjoy sports because they combine competition and physical exercise. I like to compete against other people to see if he can run as fast as someone else. You get a big thrill if you run a race and you are the first one across the finish line. In addition to competition, sports give me physical exercise. I keep my muscles strong and your heart pumping in good condition when you participate in sports. Sports are a way to push the human body to the limits of its physical capacity. When the body is tired from physical activity and you have won the race, you feel good.

Grammar Review

The following grammar points will help you write about reasons or causes. If you want to review them, turn to the pages listed below.

Using the Internet

 INTERNET ACTIVITY Choose a city that you might want to move to. Use a search engine such as Google, Yahoo!, or Excite to find Web sites about the city and do the following.

1. Find out as much information as you can about the city. For example, find out about schools, hospitals, the cost of houses, employment, transportation, museums, parks, entertainment, and the weather.
2. On another piece of paper, make a list of reasons why you would want to move there. Give specific examples and details to support each reason.
3. Explain your reasons to a partner or your classmates and teacher. While speaking, use connecting words to indicate reasons and examples.
4. When you are finished explaining your reasons, compare your reasons with your partner's or classmates'. Do you have similar reasons?
5. Your teacher may ask you to write a paragraph about why you want to move to this city.

Preparing to Write

Explaining Your Points

In analyzing, the writer must explain his or her points. The writer must show how the details and examples relate to the generalization. The writer must connect the support to the topic sentence.

Read the following paragraph. The underlined sentences help to explain the writer's point and connect the support to the generalization.

Money causes teenagers to feel stress. <u>It makes them feel bad about themselves and envy other people.</u> My friend, for instance, lives with her family and has to share a room with her sister, who is very cute and intelligent. This girl wishes she could have her own room and have a lot of stuff, <u>but she can't have these things because her family doesn't have much money. Her family's income is pretty low because her father is old and doesn't go to work. Her sister is the only one who works. Because her family can't buy her the things she wants, she feels a lot of stress and gets angry sometimes.</u> Once, she wanted a beautiful dress to wear to a sweetheart dance. She asked her sister for some money to buy the dress. She was disappointed because her sister didn't have money to give her.

She sat in silence for a little while and then started yelling out loud. She said her friends got anything they wanted but she didn't. Then she felt sorry for herself and asked why she was born into a poor family. <u>Not having money has caused this girl to think negatively about herself and her family.</u> It has caused a lot of stress in her life.

—*Ai Thianh Tran*

ACTIVITY 4-10   Following are some generalizations and examples. For each one, write a specific example. Then, write an explanation to show how your example relates to and supports the generalization. The first one is done as an example.

1. Some students fail in college because they can't handle the freedom of college life.

   a. Students don't have to go to class if they don't want to.

   b. My roommate, Eric, stays out late with his friends almost every night and then sleeps late in the morning. Since no one is there to make him go to class, he only goes to his classes when he feels like it—about once a week.

   Explanation:

   > Because he misses his classes, Eric misses important lectures and does poorly on his tests. Thus, he is failing most of his subjects. The freedom to go to class or not is part of college life, but it is a part that Eric can't handle. He doesn't have the discipline he needs to succeed in college life.

2. Adolescents disagree with their parents about their appearance.

   a. Some parents want to tell teenagers what to wear.

   b. (give a specific example) _____

   _____

   _____

   _____

   Explanation: _____

   _____

   _____

   _____

   _____

3. People exercise in order to stay healthy.

    a. One way to get exercise is to walk every day.

    b. (give a specific example) _____

_____

_____

_____

Explanation: _____

_____

_____

_____

_____

Outlining Your Points

An **outline** is the basic structure or skeleton of a piece of writing. It includes the main idea, the support, and the details. It shows the relationship of ideas.

An outline is useful in two ways. It is a good way to organize a piece of writing. A writer can use an outline as a basic plan from which to write. It is also useful to outline a paragraph or essay after it is written to make sure it is unified and coherent.

The basic method for outlining a paragraph is as follows:

Topic Sentence: Write out the topic sentence in a complete sentence.

A. Write out the first supporting point.
    1. Give a detail or example about A.
        a. Give a specific detail about 1.
    2. Give another detail about A.
    3. Give an explanation connecting the first supporting point to topic sentence if appropriate.

B. Write out the second supporting point.
    1. Give a detail or example about B.
        a. More detail.
        b. More detail.
    2. Another detail or explanation about B if appropriate.

C. Another supporting point if appropriate.

Write out the concluding sentence.

ACTIVITY 4-11   Using the form given above, outline the following paragraph.

All foreign students have the same difficulty—the English barrier. Sometimes, to make an American understand and to be able to understand Americans is not easy for a foreigner. One area of difficulty is the words of English. When I was in high school, I tried to learn as many words as I could every day. Once, I happened to use an old word which people nowadays don't use anymore and my teacher and friends couldn't understand what I said. English words also cause problems because there are a lot of words that combine to make different meanings. We have to learn how to combine words instead of trying to make sentences in our own ways. An example of combined words with different meanings is the verb-and-preposition combination, "to work out." When the word "work" goes alone, it means to work, but when it goes with the word "out," it means to exercise physically. Another difficulty for foreigners is pronunciation. English has some words that appear to be the same but have different pronunciations for different meanings. For instance, the word "conduct" has two meanings, the attitude and behavior of someone, or to lead or guide someone, depending on the pronunciation. To understand an American also depends on his or her accent. Where he or she comes from affects the accent; northerners have a different accent from southerners. If a foreigner learns English in the northern part of the country, he or she might have trouble communicating with southerners. Later on, when foreign students study in their majors, they find that they have to learn technical terms and phrases, which may be about new technology that doesn't exist in their countries. This technological language is also part of the English barrier. Many foreign students find that learning English is the hardest part of college life.

—Luan Ngo

Writing

Writing Assignment 2: Analyzing Reasons

Now you are going to write a paragraph analyzing people and their behavior.

1. PREPARE TO WRITE.

   A. First decide on a topic that you would like to analyze. Choose one of the topics below.

Reasons or Causes for the Behavior of a Group of People

Why do people (or a specific group)   exercise?

watch sports?

tell white lies?

gossip?

have conflicts?

root for the underdog?

watch horror movies?

Why do students fail in college?

Why do adolescents like   rock music?

smoke cigarettes?

Why is a particular TV show/movie/product popular?

Why is _____ a hero?

B. After you have decided on your topic, get ideas by using one of the methods given in Appendix B, pages 204–208.

C. Decide on a controlling idea and write a topic sentence.

D. Choose effective supporting points.

E. Think of details and examples to support your points.

F. Outline your paragraph in a logical way.

2. WRITE THE PARAGRAPH.

Be sure to explain your points; connect the support to the topic sentence.

3. REVISE THE PARAGRAPH.

A. Use the Revising Checklist to evaluate your paragraph, or ask a partner to do it.

B. Revise your paragraph.

Revising Checklist

1. Do you have a clear, focused generalization for a topic sentence?
2. Do you have enough details and examples to support the generalization?
3. Do all of the details and examples support the topic sentence, or are any of them off the topic?
4. Do you explain your points? Do you make the connection between the generalization and the support?

5. Do you organize the paragraph in a logical way?
6. Do you use appropriate connecting words?
7. Is the paragraph interesting?

More Reading and Writing

Discussion. Discuss these questions with your classmates or teacher.

1. Do you think teenagers feel stress? Why?
2. Do adults feel stress? Why?
3. Do you think teenagers feel more stress than adults do? Why?

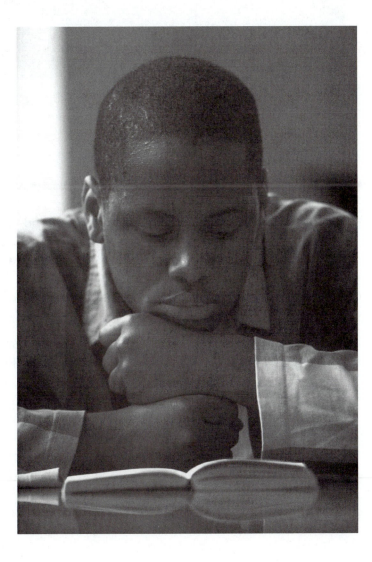

Reading

Teenagers and Stress
by David Inman

In this reading, David Inman reports on a round-table discussion sponsored by the newspaper he writes for, the *Louisville Courier-Journal*. The newspaper staff invited some local high school students to a meeting to discuss issues relevant to teenagers. In this article, the writer reports on their discussion of the causes of stress in the lives of young people.

"Sometimes I feel like adults think that teenagers don't have stress," said Amanda Wise, 15, a sophomore at Louisville Collegiate School. "They don't realize how great the pressure is."

The twelve students on The Courier-Journal High School Round Table said they have had firsthand experience with stress and see friends **grappling**° with it as well.

struggling, fighting

Two members of the panel said they've **contemplated suicide**° because of pressures at home, at school and in their personal lives. Mental health experts say suicide is the second most **prevalent**° cause of death for teenagers, second only to accidents. About 1,700 teenagers commit suicide each year in the United States.

thought about killing themselves

common

The teen panel members discussed sources of stress.

What causes stress? Stress "is your response to pressures and situations," said Miriam Vox, 17, a senior at Bowling Green High School. "It's caused by your frame of mind, telling yourself that you're not doing as well as you should."

"It's your ability or inability to cope with whatever your situation is," said Eric Douglas, 18, a senior at Corydon Central High School.

It can be **tricky**° to **pin down**° where the stress comes from, the panelists agreed.

difficult, confusing
identify exactly

"It comes from a number of sources," said Chrysti Powell, 17, a senior at Silver Creek High School in Sellersburg, Ind. "It comes from inside yourself because you want to achieve. It comes from outside, from people who want you to achieve and in some positions need you to achieve when you have some responsibility. People are depending on you and you're depending on yourself."

Drew Daniel, 16, a junior at St. Francis High School, a private school in downtown Louisville, said he feels under stress when "everybody assumes that you're not busy except for the thing they are asking you to do.

"Every teacher assumes that you don't have any other subjects. I've got a job; I'm in the play; I have a term paper; I do a magazine; I have a girlfriend; I have friends; and I have to get all A's. It's too much responsibility and people expect too much from you."

That includes going to college, of course.

"Between the college admissions people and your parents and teachers and even your peers, everyone wants to know what you are going to do with your life," said Jennifer Buehler, 17, a senior at Oldham County High School.

"When you're only 16 or 17 or 18, it's very difficult to plan out the rest of your life, especially with the changes in our society where people will probably be having many careers and having lots of different choices to make all through life, not just as a teenager."

But the panelists added that stress can often come from within.

"I have pressure from swimming and that's because I want to do well," Miriam said. "Nobody depends on me at all on my team. Because I'm not a star of the team or anything, but I just want to do well."

Pressure "can also come from your family," added Angelique David, 17, a senior at Presentation Academy.

"If you have a lot of different brothers and sisters in your family and they do well in school, then your parents for some reason sometimes expect you not to be yourself and they want you to follow in their footsteps. Then stress comes from not trying to please yourself but others—everyone else but yourself."

Can stress ever be good?

Sometimes, the panelists said.

"It can challenge you and make you push harder," Chrysti said.

"You might as well get used to facing stress now, because if you want to succeed, you're going to run into it again," said Ben Cottrell, 17, a junior at Hart County High School. "If you really want to do good, you end up bringing some of it on yourself."

Comprehension. Answer the following questions.

1. According to the panel members, what is stress?
2. What causes stress?
3. The teenagers name three places that stress comes from. What are they?

Discussion. Discuss these questions with your classmates or teacher.

1. Do you think teenagers today face a lot of stress? Do you think young adults face a lot of stress?
2. Can you think of causes for stress not mentioned in the article? What are they?
3. Can you give an example of a young person you know who faces a lot of stress? Tell how you know the person and what causes his or her stress.

Topics for Discussion and Writing

Your teacher may ask you to discuss or write about one or more of the following topics.

1. Why is a particular friend or relative always getting into trouble?
2. At what age should a person start working for pay, and why?
3. Why would a man or woman enter a field that has traditionally been filled by the opposite sex, such as nursing or engineering?
4. Why is soccer popular around the world but not in the United States?
5. Why is a particular social policy in your country popular or unpopular?
6. Why are educated citizens important in a democracy?

Chapter 5 Analyzing Processes

Theme

Living with Computers

Goals

Writing

To write a paragraph analyzing a process

To give all the necessary steps in the process

To organize by chronological order

To improve cohesion by using connecting words for process analysis

Reading

To read about and analyze processes

Grammar

To review passive voice

To review gerunds and infinitives

Getting Started

Journal Writing: How To Do a Simple Operation on a Computer

Computers are part of our daily lives. We use them at the bank, at the library, at home, and at work. We all need to know how to use them. Imagine that you are going to tell someone how to do a simple operation on a computer, like logging on, cutting and pasting, or sending e-mail. In your journal, write the steps that tell how to do this operation. Answer the following questions.

1. What is the operation you are explaining?
2. What is the first step in the process?
3. The second?
4. The next?
5. The next?

(If you prefer, tell how to use another piece of equipment, such as a boat, a VCR, a can opener, or a sewing machine.)

Discussion. Tell your classmates or teacher the steps in the process you wrote about.

CNN®Video Activity: Cyber College Counsel

 Universities use computers for many reasons. For example, students can register for classes or look up their grades on computers. The video describes a helpful computer system called ISIS (Integrated Student Information Service), which is used by students at the University of Florida.

Before you watch the video, discuss these questions with your classmates or teacher.

1. Does your school or university have a computer system for students to register for classes and/or find out their grades? If so, what is the system called?
2. Does your school have a Web site? If so, what kinds of information can you find there?
3. What services would you like the computer system on your campus to add?

Understanding the Video

Comprehension. Before you watch the video, read the statements below. As you watch the video, put a *T* for *True* or an *F* for *False* next to the following statements about ISIS. After you watch the video, answer the questions.

1. Students can look up information about their grades, financial aid packages, and transcripts.
2. Students can only use the ISIS at certain times during registration.
3. Students need one number, their PIN number, to log on to ISIS.
4. Universal Tracking lets students know exactly what courses they need to graduate on time.
5. "Major shopping" on ISIS showed one student in the video that he would lose ground if he changed from one computer specialty to another.
6. The "retention rate" (the percentage of students who stay in school and do not drop out) at the University of Florida is approaching 90 percent.
7. Thirty-five thousand students attend the University of Florida.

Discussion. After you watch the video, discuss these questions with your classmates or teacher.

1. What features of ISIS do you think are the most helpful?
2. How does ISIS keep students from dropping out of college?
3. Can you imagine any problems using a computerized system like ISIS?
4. Could your college or university benefit from using ISIS or a system like it? If so, in what ways?

Reading

Discuss these questions with your classmates or teacher.

1. Look at the photograph on page 100. Where are the people in the picture?
2. What do you think they are doing?
3. If you go to your library, what resources are available on computer?

Reading

OPAC at the Earl K. Long Library
by Hsin-Chuan Chen

This essay was written by Hsin-Chuan Chen when he was studying accounting at the University of New Orleans. He wrote this essay when he was a student in an ESL class.

"OPAC? What is that?" Maybe this is a question you have asked. People, including me, have gone to the library to study many times, but they have never used OPAC (Online Public **Access°** Catalog) to look for books in the library. Many people know of such a system, but they don't know

entrance, admission

how to use it. In fact, you don't need to worry about it if you aren't good at operating a computer because it is easy to use. All I can say about OPAC in one word is that it is convenient.

You don't need anything to use OPAC; you just go to one of the monitors located on the first floor of the library and you can begin your search. First of all, if the monitor of the computer is blank, you can press any key, and the monitor turns to the main screen. Or you can press F2 to clear any old searches. At once, the monitor shows "Welcome to LOUIS" (Louisiana Online University Information System). It lists all the names of the libraries at the public colleges and universities in Louisiana. When you have done this, all you need to do is type the three-letter code for the library you want. For example, you type "UNO" (for University of New Orleans). Then, the monitor shows "Welcome to LAFITTE," which is the name of OPAC at UNO. Now you can use five ways to look for the book you want. They are by author, title, subject, keyword, and call number.

If you know the name of the author, for instance, George P. Oslin, you can type "a=Oslin, George P.," being sure to put the last name first. Then, the monitor will show all the titles of the books which this author has written. You can choose a book by pressing the number which is associated with it, and get the following information: location, where the book is in the library; call number, the indexing number of the book; and status, whether the book is in the library or not.

If you know the title of the book, for instance, *Clint,* you can type "t=clint" directly. Then you can get the information about the book. If there are some books with the same title, the monitor will show all the names of the authors so you can tell which book is the one you are looking for. You use this same search procedure if you want to look for a book by subject, key word, or call number.

Even though all this is easy to use, you also need to know some commands. One useful command is "hel," which means help. Whenever you need to continue the process, you can type "hel." Then the monitor shows you what to do for the next step. "Lon" means long view. If you type "lon," you can get more details about the book you want. Other commands are "sta," which means to go back to the main menu and "oth," which means other options. If you want to change the way you are looking for a book, you can type "oth." If you want to change libraries in the middle of a search, you can type "cho."

Compared with the old card catalog system, OPAC is really convenient for people who want to look for books in the library. To your surprise, all you need to do is to pay attention to the directions on the monitor. Once you use OPAC, you will be satisfied that it is convenient.

Comprehension. Answer the following questions.

1. What is OPAC? What is its purpose?
2. What is the first step in using OPAC?
3. What do you choose when the monitor says "Welcome to LOUIS"?

4. What comes on the screen when you choose "UNO"?

5. What are the five ways you can search for a book?

6. What do the following commands mean? When do you use them?
   "hel"
   "lon"
   "sta"
   "oth"
   "cho"

7. What is the writer's opinion about OPAC?

Discussion. Discuss these questions with your classmates or teacher.

1. Do you know how to use the computer search system at your library? If so, is it the same or different from the one Chen describes? Explain the differences.

2. What are some of the advantages of this kind of computer search system?

3. Are there any disadvantages? What are they?

NOTE: If you want to read another essay analyzing a process, read "Map your Tongue" by Eric Haseltine on pages 114–115.

Preparing to Write

Analyzing a Process

One way to analyze something is to look at it as a **process.** In describing a process, we break something into a series of connected steps. For example, we can look at writing a paragraph as a process, or series of steps. First, you get ideas, then you focus on a main idea, then you gather support, next you think about organization, and finally you write the paragraph. Breaking an activity into the steps of a process is a useful way to analyze because we can see each part clearly and focus on one part at a time.

Academic writing and writing at work often call for analyzing processes. For example, a lab report in chemistry, a memo to sales associates, or instructions for assembling a product all require process writing.

Supporting with a Process

A paragraph describing a process tells how to do something. Often the writer imagines that the audience does not know how to do something and it is his or her job to teach or explain how to carry out each step in the process. Thus, the support for a process paragraph is the steps in the process. Following are some guidelines for you in analyzing a process.

A. Be aware of your audience. Think about who your readers are and how much they know about the process you are going to describe. Your readers' background and knowledge will determine how much you need to explain. Imagine that you are going to explain how to use a library computer search system. If your readers have never used a computer before, you will need to give more details than if your readers are familiar with how to use a computer.

ACTIVITY 5-1   Imagine that you are going to explain how to register for classes at your school to a group of international students. Answer these questions about your audience.

1. What do they probably know about the topic?
2. Are most of them familiar with this process?
3. What differences might there be between the process in this country and in their home country?

B. Give all the necessary steps in the process. Make sure the process is complete. Do not leave out important steps. Again, imagine that you are going to explain how to register for classes at your school to a group of international students. Following is a list of steps. Is it complete?

1. Go to your college office.
2. At your college office, you will first pick up your registration materials.
3. Then, you will go to see your advisor.
4. After that, you will make out your schedule.
5. Finally, you will pay your fees.

Your readers might have some questions about the process. For example, they may ask how do I know which is my college? Do I need to take anything with me? How do I know who my advisor is?

ACTIVITY 5-2   With your teacher and classmates, make a list of questions international students might ask about how to register for classes at your school.

ACTIVITY 5-3   With your teacher and classmates, answer the questions you wrote in Activity 5-2 and make some notes of the answers.

ACTIVITY 5-4   Rewrite the list of steps given above about how to register for classes at your school, making it more complete. Use the information you discussed in Activity 5-3.

C. Explain or describe the materials or equipment required. If there is equipment the reader is not familiar with, explain it. For example, if you are going to tell how to play games on the computer, you will have to explain what equipment is necessary.

ACTIVITY 5-5   Look at the list you wrote in Activity 5-4. Make a list of the materials students must have before they can begin the process.

D. Warn the reader of difficulties.   If there is a point where beginners can easily go wrong, warn the reader of that point. For instance, if you are telling how to use a VCR, you should warn the reader that the programming may be lost if the electrical power goes out.

ACTIVITY 5-6   Look again at the list you wrote in Activity 5-4. Decide at which point your reader might have difficulties. Mark those points. Then write sentences to explain the difficulties and what the reader should do.

E. Give details and examples to make the process clear and interesting.   You may want to take a hypothetical example and carry it through each step of the process. If you are telling how to hook up a personal computer, you might take a particular computer and use it as an example for each step of the process.

Focusing on a Main Idea

The main idea for a process paragraph may be a simple, factual statement like "There are three major steps involved in learning to use word processing." However, it is more interesting for the reader if the writer takes a persuasive point of view like "Using OPAC is convenient." In this case, the writer will show by explaining the steps of the process how convenient it is to use a library computer search system. The controlling idea, "convenient," gives coherence and focus to the paragraph or essay.

ACTIVITY 5-7   Look again at the notes you wrote about the process of registering for classes at your school. Decide on a controlling idea and write a topic sentence.

Introducing the Process

The introductory sentences of a process paragraph should introduce the process and the controlling idea. Because these sentences are the first ones the reader sees, they should also be interesting. They should make the reader want to finish reading the paragraph.

There are a number of ways to make the introductory sentences inviting to the reader. Here are some suggestions:

1. Ask a question.
2. Tell a short narrative or story.
3. Show the importance of the process.

4. Describe a common experience.
5. Use a quotation.

ACTIVITY 5-8 Reread the introductory paragraph of the reading on page 99–101. Answer the following questions.

1. What is the topic?
2. What is the controlling idea?
3. What approach (numbers 1–5 above) does the writer use to catch the reader's interest?

ACTIVITY 5-9 Read the following introductory sentences and answer the questions that follow.

1.   Do you like movies? You do? Especially good ones, right? Good! But have you ever thought about making your own movie? No? That's too bad. It's not so hard to make a movie and I'm sure you are going to love it, but first you need to know a few things.

—*Ditmar Hospital*

a. What is the topic? _____

b. What is the controlling idea? _____

c. What approach does the writer use to catch the reader's interest? _____

_____

2.   Nowadays, a lot of people have computers in their homes or offices. They are also found in large companies and government offices. These computers don't work separately; they are connected with each other with a connector, so everyone can reach his friend's computer. How are these computers connected? They are connected with a big computer network called the Internet.

—*Ali Al-Ghamdi*

a. What is the topic? _____

b. What is the controlling idea? _____

c. What approach(es) does the writer use to catch the reader's interest?

_____

3.   "It will cost you seventy dollars to get a tune-up for your car," the mechanic said when I took my car to the shop. That is too much for this job, I thought. Changing the spark plugs, checking the electrical wires, adjusting the carburetor, measuring the voltage of the battery, and checking the inflation pressure of the tires are all part of tuning

up a car. All these jobs do not take more than thirty minutes, and you can do them easily yourself.

—*Ali Al-Ghamdi*

a. What is the topic? _____

b. What is the controlling idea?_____

c. What approach does the writer use to catch the reader's interest?_____

_____

4. Bill Gates, chairman of the Microsoft Corporation, says in his book, *The Road Ahead,* "It's a great time to be alive." Gates is referring to the coming of the information revolution, in which the ways we get and send information will change dramatically. Everyone will be connected via computers and huge amounts of information will be at our fingertips. To take advantage of the information revolution, however, everyone must know how to operate a computer. As incredible as it seems, there are still some people who are not familiar with the functions of a computer. With the new user-friendly computer models, learning how to use a computer is easy.

a. What is the topic? _____

b. What is the controlling idea?_____

c. What approach does the writer use to catch the reader's interest?_____

_____

Organizing by Chronological Order

In giving the steps in a process, the writer starts with the first step and carries through to the last one. Thus, chronological order is typical in organizing the process paragraph. (For a review of chronological order, see Chapter 2, pp. 38–39.)

ACTIVITY 5-10   Read the following paragraph written by a student and answer the questions that follow.

How to Prepare for a Race

Maybe you say to yourself that you do not have to prepare for a race, that you can just go to the starting line and begin to run. But if you ask some athletes, they will tell you that you have to be prepared for the race. It means that you have to warm up and stretch all your muscles. If you do not **warm up,**° you can injure yourself; you may pull a muscle or tendon. It is good to start warming up at least forty minutes before the race. All athletes usually warm up at the stadium

prepare the body for physical activity

racers who run in
short, very fast
races

where they are going to compete or in a nearby stadium which is set
for warming up. They wear a tracksuit and a jacket because they need
to keep their muscles warm. First of all, you should start with jogging.
When you jog you run slowly, so you will not put too much strain on
your muscles in the beginning. You should run at least ten minutes,
but the length depends on the length of the race in which you will
compete. Of course long-distance runners will jog longer than **sprinters.**° For example, runners who run ten-kilometer races will jog five

kilometers to warm up, but sprinters may only jog one kilometer. However, it depends on the individual person. For example, when I run the eight hundred meter race, I jog two kilometers. Secondly, you have to stretch your muscles with different exercises. Runners pay the most attention to exercises for their legs. They have to stretch all their leg muscles. For example, a good exercise to stretch the Achilles tendon is to stand facing a wall and push against it with both hands. Straighten one leg out behind you and push. Then change legs, straighten out the other leg, and push. After you have exercised all your muscles, you can move on to the next step. The third step to warming up is to run really fast, as fast as you will run in the real race. Usually you do this for no more than one hundred meters, but you will repeat this fast running for maybe three times. This running fast starts the body and gets it ready for the real race. Warming up is very important. It is the first step to winning.

—*Renata Strakova*

1. What process does the writer describe?
2. Does she have a persuasive controlling idea?
3. Does she give all the necessary steps in the process? What are they? Does she leave out any steps? What are they?
4. Does she tell what equipment is needed? What is it?
5. Does she warn the reader of difficulties?
6. Does she give examples and details? What are they?
7. Does the writer have an interesting introduction?

ACTIVITY 5-11　Review your notes and topic sentence about how to register at your school and write a paragraph.

Using Language Effectively

Cohesion: Connecting Words for Process Analysis

In Chapter 2, you studied connecting words to use with narrative writing. Both narrative and process are organized according to chronological order. Therefore, you will use the same connecting words to indicate process as you did to signal narrative. You will use subordinators in adverbial clauses of time and transitional words to indicate sequence.

WORDS TO INDICATE TIME RELATIONSHIPS

SUBORDINATORS

while	before	the moment that
when	after	once
as	until	
whenever	as soon as	

Examples

When you have done this, all you need to do is just type the three-letter code for the library you want.

Whenever you need to continue the process, you can type "hel."

Once you use OPAC, you will be satisfied that it is convenient.

WORDS TO INDICATE SEQUENCE

TRANSITIONAL WORDS

first, second, etc.	at once	last
first of all	right away	finally
next	then	

Examples

First of all, if the monitor is blank, you can press any key.

Then, the monitor will show all the titles of the books which this author has written.

ACTIVITY 5-12   Read the following essay and do the following activities.

How To Operate a Restaurant Computer

Many people line up to wait for a good dinner in a Chinese restaurant. While they are waiting patiently, the hostesses are busy greeting other customers and the waiters are busy serving others. To help the high efficiency of the service, the waiters use a computer to organize everything, such as drink orders, food orders, and checks. This computer, which is simpler than other ones, is only used in a restaurant. To learn how to operate this computer, you don't need any technical knowledge of computers. The equipment that you need includes the computer itself, a small screen similar to a TV screen that gives instructions which tell you what to do, and a small printer.

When all the equipment is properly set up, you can begin. First, you put your server number into the computer; then you have to begin the table. For example, the hostess brings you two customers at table six. At this moment, to begin the table, you press the button "t," which stands for "table," and number 6. After this, the computer asks you how many guests there are and you press 2. Let's assume you already took their orders. Now, you should press the "menu" buttons for orders. First, you press the "drink" button to get them some drinks. If they order two Cokes, you press the "soft drinks" button to get two Cokes. If they order two egg rolls, which are appetizers, you press the "appetizer" button to get them the egg rolls. After you have pressed the "drink" and "appetizer" buttons, you press the "send in" button, which will automatically send the order to the kitchen and bar; otherwise the cook and the bartender don't know what you want.

When the customers are almost finished with their appetizers, you press in that table again, and then press the menu button to order the main entrees for them. For example, if they have one order of sweet and sour pork and one order of Peking duck, you press the "pork" button and the "duck" button. Don't forget to press the "send in" button. If you press a wrong order by accident, press the cancel button to void it.

After the customers have finished their dinner, you should press the "check" button for that table so the computer will print out the check. The check will have a list of all the food and drinks they ordered and the total on it. Through all these steps, you will find out that using a restaurant computer is quite simple, and fun too.

—*Mo Fung (Jackie) Chan*

1. List all the adverbial clauses of time that give cohesion to the essay.

   _____

   _____

   _____

2. List the words indicating sequence.

_____

_____

_____

_____

3. What other connecting words does the writer use? List them here.

_____

_____

_____

_____

Grammar Review

The following grammar points will help you write process analysis. If you want to review them, turn to the pages listed below.

Passive Voice   Page 243
Gerunds and Infinitives   Page 245

Using the Internet

 INTERNET ACTIVITY   Many Web sites give "how to" information. For example, you can find out how to tie a tie, how to put up a tent, or how to make a cake. Use a search engine such as Google, Yahoo!, or Excite to find a Web site that tells how to do something, and do the following.

1. On a separate sheet of paper, make a list of the steps in the process.
2. Decide if the steps in the process are complete. If not, can you add information to complete the process?
3. Explain your process to a partner or your classmates and teacher. While speaking, use connecting words to indicate process analysis.
4. Ask your partner or classmates if the process is complete. If it is not, ask for help to complete the process.
5. Your teacher may ask you to write a paragraph analyzing the process.

Writing: Analyzing a Process

Writing Assignment

Now you are going to write a paragraph analyzing a process.

1. PREPARE TO WRITE.

   A. First, think of a topic. Choose a process that you are very familiar with, something you know how to do well. Here are some suggestions.

   How To Do a Particular Operation on a Home or School Computer:

   > How to log on
   >
   > How to use a search engine
   >
   > How to cut and paste
   >
   > How to make charts and graphs
   >
   > How to play a game
   >
   > How to play music
   >
   > How to find information in an encyclopedia
   >
   > How to send e-mail

   Other processes:

   > How to use a particular machine
   >
   > How to make a videotape
   >
   > How to perform a magic trick
   >
   > How to play a particular game
   >
   > How to plan a party
   >
   > How to cope with a bad boss
   >
   > How to succeed in a particular course
   >
   > How to climb a mountain
   >
   > How to learn a foreign language
   >
   > How to make new friends
   >
   > How to get through registration at your school

   B. After you have decided on your topic, get ideas by using one of the methods given in Appendix B, pp. 204–208. You may want to make a list and then check the list to make sure you have included all the steps.

   C. Think about your audience. How much do they know about your topic and how much will you need to tell them?

D. In thinking about the steps in the process, be sure to do the following:

make the process complete

define and explain unfamiliar terms

warn the reader of difficulties

give examples and details

organize them chronologically

E. Decide on a controlling idea and write a topic sentence.

F. Think of an interesting way to begin your paragraph.

2. WRITE THE PARAGRAPH.

3. REVISE THE PARAGRAPH.

A. Ask a partner to evaluate your paper using the Paragraph Guidelines, or do it yourself using the Revising Checklist.

B. Revise your paragraph.

Paragraph Guidelines

1. Write out the topic sentence and circle the controlling idea.
2. List the steps in the process.
3. Does the writer have a clear topic sentence and controlling idea?
4. Does the controlling idea show the writer's attitude?
5. Does the writer do the following?
   give all the necessary steps in the process
   define and explain unfamiliar terms
   warn the reader of difficulties
   use examples and details
   organize the steps chronologically
6. Are the introductory sentences interesting? Do they make you want to finish reading the paragraph?
7. What part of the paragraph did you enjoy the most?
8. What part would you like to know more about?

Revising Checklist

1. Do you tell how to do something (analyze a process)?
2. Do you have a clear topic sentence and controlling idea?
3. Does the controlling idea show your attitude?
4. Do you do the following?
   give all the necessary steps in the process
   define and explain unfamiliar terms
   warn the reader of difficulties

use example and details
organize the steps chronologically

5. Are the introductory sentences interesting? Will they make the reader want to finish reading the paragraph?

More Reading and Writing

Discuss these questions with your classmates or teacher.

1. Do some people taste food more intensely than others?
2. How could you find out?
3. In what way are scientists like explorers of new places?

Reading

Map Your Tongue
by Eric Haseltine

This article was written by Eric Haseltine and published in the magazine *Discover* in February 2000. *Discover* is a magazine for people who are interested in science and technology.

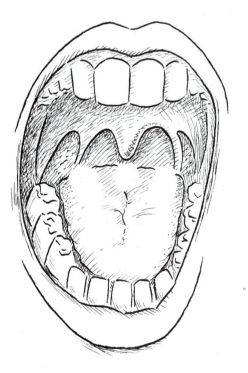

hard-to-find places
hard to find

numbers of items
in a given area

journey of
discovery

prove that
something is true

Restless? Hungry for adventure? Follow me on a thrilling journey of discovery to the **inner reaches**° of your mouth. There we shall hunt the **elusive**° taste receptor, and we'll investigate rumors that these highly specialized nerve cells, which transmit chemical information to the brain, show up in greater numbers and **densities**° in some mouths.

For the **expedition,**° you'll need a few friends, a flashlight, a magnifying glass, a vial of blue food coloring, and some cotton swabs. Also, bring salt and plenty of fresh water.

Now, on to the experiments.

EXPERIMENT 1. Early explorers found taste receptors more populous in some regions of the tongue than in others. To **confirm**° this, wet the end of a swab, roll it in a pile of salt, and probe the tip, center, sides, and the very back of the tongue, rinsing between touches. The intensity of taste, which is roughly proportional to the number of receptors, will vary considerably depending on the spot. The front of your tongue should register a far greater reaction than the middle. Now, with a new dab of salt on the swab, probe the back of your palate and around the inside of your mouth. You should discover taste receptors dwelling on the roof of your mouth. They're in the esophagus too. (But don't venture there. That territory is patrolled by the gag reflex.)

EXPERIMENT 2. Sprinkle a few drops of blue food coloring onto your tongue. Gently rub in the color with a clean swab and inspect the results in the mirror using the flashlight and magnifying glass. You should see pale, mushroomlike structures called *fungiform papillae*—home to your taste buds—floating in a sea of blue. These little bumps each contain hundreds of taste-receptor cells. Compare the numbers of papillae at the tip of your tongue with those in the middle. Now make your friends paint their tongues blue and compare papillae densities. About 25 percent of us qualify as supertasters because our tongues are tightly packed with taste buds. Another 25 percent are nontasters, with fewer and more sparsely distributed papillae. The rest of us fall in between.

With a magnifying glass in hand and a blue tongue, explore your mouth and seek your destiny. Want to know more? Go to www .discover.com/brainworks.

Comprehension. Answer the following questions.

1. What is a taste receptor? What does a taste receptor do?
2. What equipment do you need for the experiments?
3. What is Experiment 1 trying to prove?
4. How do you carry out Experiment 1?

5. What should be the results of Experiment 1?
6. What parts of the mouth besides the tongue have taste receptors?
7. What are fungiform papillae?
8. What is Experiment 2 trying to prove?
9. How do you carry out Experiment 2?
10. What should be the results of Experiment 2?

Discussion. Discuss these questions with your classmates or teacher.

1. What comparison does the writer use throughout the article? Find words and phrases showing this comparison. Is the comparison interesting?
2. What is the writer's attitude toward his topic?
3. Do you think you are a supertaster, a nontaster, or a normal taster? Why do you think so?

Topics for Discussion and Writing

Your teacher may ask you to discuss or write about one of the following topics.

1. Analyze how to do a simple science experiment.
2. Analyze how to prepare for a journey of exploration to a place you have never been.
3. Analyze how to bargain for a car in the United States or for some item in your culture.
4. Analyze how to make a complaint about a purchase.
5. Analyze how to build a fire in a fireplace or outside at a campfire.
6. Analyze how to catch fish or crabs.
7. Analyze how to relax.

Chapter **6** **Comparing and Contrasting**

Theme

Education

Goals

Writing

To write a paragraph comparing or contrasting two aspects of education

To find points of comparison

To organize by points or subjects

To improve cohesion by using connecting words for comparison and contrast

To contrast "then" and "now"

Reading

To read about differences in education

Grammar

To review comparative forms

To review correlative conjunctions

To review run-on sentences and comma splices

Getting Started

Journal Writing: Two Aspects of My Education

How many schools have you attended in your life? Think about the schools you have attended and choose one of these topics to write about.

two high schools
two colleges
two teachers of the same subject
two courses of the same subject

Answer the following questions:

1. What do you remember about the two things? List the ideas that come to mind.

   Example

MUSCODA HIGH SCHOOL	NASHUA HIGH SCHOOL
couldn't study foreign language	studied French
students were friendly	students not so friendly
had lots of dances, student activities	didn't have many dances

2. Look at your lists. From the ideas on your lists, what generalizations can you make about the two items? Write several generalizations.

   Examples of generalizations:
   Nashua High School offered a greater variety of courses.
   Muscoda High School offered a better social life.

Discussion. Discuss your generalizations with your classmates or teacher. Be prepared to support your generalizations with examples.

CNN® Video Activity: Home School College

Home schooling is becoming more common in the United States, although the number of students who are educated at home is still small. The video shows some home-schooled students that are attending Piedmont College in Georgia.

Before you watch the video, discuss these questions with your classmates or teacher.

1. What are the advantages of staying home to learn school subjects from parents instead of going to a school?
2. What are the disadvantages of home schooling?
3. Are most parents qualified to teach their children all the subjects that are required in schools?

Understanding the Video

Comprehension. Read the following questions. As you watch the video, take brief notes. After you watch the video, answer the questions.

1. How many home-schoolers go to Piedmont College?
2. Why does Piedmont College recruit home-schoolers?
3. In what ways does Matt Martin think he has an advantage over students who are not schooled at home?
4. How many home-schoolers are now in colleges and universities in the United States?
5. Is it easier or harder for home-schoolers to get into colleges and universities? Why?
6. What job did Matt Martin's mother have before she home-schooled her children?

Discussion. After you watch the video, discuss these questions with your classmates or teacher.

1. Why do some parents prefer to teach their own children at home?
2. One young woman in the video says she had an active social life in high school even though she was home-schooled. Do you think some home-schooled students miss out on the social life that school provides? Why or why not?
3. Do the advantages of home-schooling outweigh the disadvantages?
4. Would you have preferred to be home-schooled as a child?

Reading

Discuss these questions with your classmates or teacher.

1. What do you know about Moscow high schools?
2. What do you think a Russian high school student would think of an American high school?

Reading

Notes from an American School
by Artyom Aslanyan

This essay was written by Artyom Aslanyan, a ninth-grader at Moscow School No. 20. It was published in *Soviet Life* in August 1989.

Last February the *Seattle Times* called me "a walking advertisement for **détente.**"° At that time I was visiting the United States on a month-long educational exchange, along with fourteen of my classmates and teachers.

a decrease in the tensions between two countries

In Seattle we stayed with local families and went to the Lakeside School, which has maintained friendly relations with my school for ten years now. Over the past few years we in Moscow have hosted several groups of American students. Now it was our turn to visit them.

Classes were hard at first, although the atmosphere was relaxed and friendly. On our first day at Lakeside we were shocked to see a boy in ragged jeans eating a sandwich and drinking juice right in the middle of a lesson, while listening to the teacher and taking notes in his notebook. The classroom, too, was very different from what we were used to. All the tables were arranged in a circle. It was sometimes hard to say who was a teacher and who was a student.*

standards of right and wrong

After hearing all sorts of rumors about **morals**° in the United States, we were pleasantly surprised to see how polite all of the students, including the youngest, were. In a school on Shaw Island, near Seattle, we watched three juniors playing a computer game. I volunteered to play with them. One of the boys politely told me that he would be willing to let me take his place.

known; famous

Lakeside School is **distinguished**° not only for its special teacher-student relationship but also for its high technical standards. There is nothing in our school that comes anywhere close to what we saw in some of the American classrooms. For instance, students were given a video camera and instructed to shoot a movie before the class met again.

necessary; required

The range of courses that American students have to choose from is stupendous. Aside from the **mandatory**° courses, students at Lakeside can pick out a number of elective classes that interest them and can challenge themselves in these fields. I think this makes it possible for students to learn what their talents and **inclinations**° are and to make the right choice for the future. But even with all these extra options, American students have more free time than we do.

interests; likings

A lot of what we've seen in the American school could be used by the Soviet school system in its efforts to democratize the teaching process, create a freer atmosphere, establish better student-teacher relationships, and most important of all, improve the quality of education. True, in the United States some parents pay more than 400 dollars a month for the education of their son or daughter in a private school, while tuition is free for all students in the Soviet Union. But many people in the USSR

---

* Editor's note: In Moscow's schools, male teachers, especially young ones, are very rare.

standards of right
and wrong;
morality

now say that free tuition and free health care aren't adequate to cover society's present needs. I would say that our Soviet schools teach many subjects in greater depth than the American schools do. But American schools teach some subjects—**ethics,**° for instance—that aren't taught at all in our school.

Comprehension. Answer the following questions.

1. Under what arrangement was Aslanyan studying in an American school?
2. Aslanyan gives a number of differences between Lakeside School and his school in Moscow. List as many differences as you can.
3. In paragraph four, Aslanyan tells about a difference between what he had expected and what he found. Explain the difference.
4. Why does Aslanyan think elective courses are a good idea?
5. According to Aslanyan, what are some of the positive aspects of American schools? Of Russian schools?
6. According to Aslanyan, what are some of the negative aspects of American schools? Of Russian schools?
7. What is Aslanyan's main idea? Summarize it in one sentence.

Discussion. Discuss these questions with your classmates or teacher.

1. Discuss the similarities and differences between education in the United States and education in your country.
2. What expectations did you have before you came to this school? Have your expectations been fulfilled? Was there a difference between your expectations and reality?
3. What do you think would be the perfect high school?

NOTE: If you want to read another article showing comparison and contrast, read "Literacy Around the World," on pages 139–141.

Preparing to Write

Focusing on a Main Idea

One way to analyze something is to compare or contrast it with a comparable thing. **To compare** means to show the similarities and **to contrast** means to show the differences. In university classes, you may contrast two famous people, a country before and after an important historical event, or two scientific theories. In everyday life, you compare and contrast when you buy a car or choose an apartment. When you compare and contrast two things, you can understand them better.

In comparing and contrasting, the writer is often trying to determine which of two items is better or preferable. In the paragraphs you write, you should focus on either comparing or contrasting so that you can develop one idea fully.

The main idea of a comparison/contrast paragraph should show the writer's attitude, opinion, or idea. A simple, factual statement like "There are two major differences between the two teachers" is not very interesting. It is more interesting for the reader if the writer takes a persuasive point of view, such as "Ms. Smith has a better teaching method than Mr. White." In this case, the writer will focus on teaching methods and show how one is better than the other. The controlling idea, "better teaching method," gives coherence and focus to the paragraph.

ACTIVITY 6-1   Read the following paragraph written by a student. Underline the topic sentence and circle the controlling idea.

Two Teachers

More than fifty teachers taught me during my thirteen years in high school. I don't remember any of them except two, Ali and Ahmad. Both of them were Egyptian and taught math. Ali taught me in sixth grade and Ahmad taught me in seventh grade. They were well-known teachers in the school. Ali was hated by many students, but Ahmad was a good teacher and a lot of students liked him. The differences between these teachers were attitude and teaching method. The worst math class I ever had was in sixth grade when Ali was the teacher. His attitude was very bad. Basically, he was lazy. He didn't give us any homework because he didn't want to correct it. In contrast with Ali, Ahmad was the best teacher in the school. When he taught me in the seventh grade, I got full marks because I understood everything he taught. His attitude about the students was very good. He made his students like him because he believed that if students like the teacher, they will like his class and will do their best to satisfy the teacher. Ali also had a bad method of teaching. He just sat down on the desk in front of the class and read the book. After he finished reading, he asked if there were any questions. Then he sat down until the class time was over. Once one of my friends told him that we didn't understand anything from the reading and that he should explain the lesson on the blackboard. Ali replied, "I am just responsible to teach you what is in the book and I can do no more." Unlike Ali's teaching method, the teaching method Ahmad used was very good; all the students liked it. Ahmad began the class with a review of the last lesson, to make sure we understood the lesson. Then he began to explain the new lesson on the blackboard several times. Because of his method, it was easy to understand the lesson. A year later, Ali quit teaching and went to work in a private company; Ahmad is the manager of the best school in my city.

—*Abdullah Al-Shamisi*

Choosing Comparable Items

When a writer compares or contrasts, he or she must choose two comparable items. They must be of the same general class. The writer can compare two math teachers or two English classes but it would not be fair (or interesting) to compare an elementary school and a university.

ACTIVITY 6-2   Write the names of two comparable items for each of the groups below. Discuss with your teacher or classmates why your examples can be compared.

1. two teachers _____

2. two classes _____

3. two textbooks _____

4. two vocational schools _____

5. two universities _____

6. two university bookstores _____

7. two dormitories _____

Finding Points of Comparison

In comparing or contrasting two things, the writer needs to use the same points of support for both things. For example, in the paragraph, "Two Teachers," the writer used two points of comparison: attitude and method of teaching. For some topics, there are many points of comparison a writer could use. Generally, the writer chooses the points that are the most important and interesting.

ACTIVITY 6-3   Following is a list of features about two universities. The features have been grouped together under points of comparison. Name the points of comparison. The first one is done as an example.

TWO UNIVERSITIES

UNIVERSITY A	UNIVERSITY B
1. *Admission Requirements*	
ACT score of 21	Rank in upper half of high school class
or	or
TOEFL score of 500	TOEFL score of 550
2.	
Tuition	Tuition
Residents $1,481	Residents $2,991
Nonresidents $3,257	Nonresidents $7,097
Room and Board $3,580	Room and Board $3,315
Books $ 700	Books $700
3.	
6 sports clubs	14 sports clubs
Jazz band	Jazz band
International Student Org.	International Student Org.
	Football team
Basketball team	Basketball team
	Student radio station
	Foreign film series
4.	
In southern U.S.	In northern U.S.—Midwest
In city of 500,000	In city of 40,000
5.	
16,000 students	13,000 students
6.	
350 acres	750 acres
30 principal buildings	40 principal buildings

ACTIVITY 6-4   Study the information about the two universities. Which one would you rather go to? Write a topic sentence with a controlling idea that gives your choice.

Organizing by Points

One way to organize a paragraph of comparison or contrast is by **points.** In this method of organization, the writer uses the points of comparison to structure the paragraph. He or she discusses each point, giving the contrast between the two subjects. Look at the following example of a point paragraph outline.

Topic Sentence: Ali was hated by many students, but Ahmad was a good teacher and a lot of students liked him.

1. Attitude
   a. Ali
   b. Ahmad

2. Teaching Method
   a. Ali
   b. Ahmad

ACTIVITY 6-5   Using the topic sentence you wrote in Activity 6-4, write an outline for a paragraph organized by points.

ACTIVITY 6-6   Write the paragraph you outlined in Activity 6-5.

Writing

Writing Assignment 1: Comparing and Contrasting

Now you are going to write a paragraph comparing or contrasting two aspects of education. (You can choose another topic if your teacher agrees.)

1. PREPARE TO WRITE.
   A. First, think about a topic. You may choose one of the topics listed below.

   Some Aspect of Education

   Two elementary schools

   Two high schools

   A private school and a public school

Two teachers

Two campus bookstores

Two classes of the same subject

Two English programs

Two universities

Two attitudes about school

Other Topics

Two products, appliances, pieces of machinery

Two places

Two people

Two attitudes toward money, dating, clothes

B. After you have decided on your topic, get ideas by using one of the methods given in Appendix B. You may want to make a Venn diagram or brainstorm.

C. Make a list of ideas about the two things you are comparing/contrasting.

D. Look over your list and group the features into points of comparison or contrast.

E. Decide on a controlling idea.

F. Write an outline in which you organize your ideas by points.

2. WRITE THE PARAGRAPH.

3. REVISE THE PARAGRAPH.

A. Ask a partner to evaluate your paragraph using the Paragraph Guidelines, or do it yourself using the Revising Checklist.

B. Revise your paragraph.

Paragraph Guidelines
1. Write out the topic sentence.
2. Circle the controlling idea.
3. Is the topic sentence persuasive? Does it tell the writer's attitude?
4. List the points of comparison.
5. Are the points of comparison significant and interesting?
6. Is there enough support for the points?
7. Is the paragraph organized by points?
8. What part of the paragraph did you enjoy most?
9. What part would you like to know more about?

Revising Checklist

1. Do you have a clear topic sentence and controlling idea?
2. Is your topic sentence persuasive? Does it tell your attitude?
3. Do you have several points of comparison?
4. Are the points of comparison significant and interesting?
5. Do you have enough support for your points? Do you give examples and details?
6. Do you organize the paragraph by points?
7. Is the paragraph interesting?

Using Language Effectively

Cohesion: Connecting Words for Comparison and Contrast*

The connecting words below will give cohesion to your paragraph. Look at these sentences to see the appropriate sentence structure and punctuation for each kind of connecting word.

Key Words

Unlike Russian high schools, American high schools offer elective subjects.

Coordinators

American high schools offer elective subjects, **but** Russian high schools do not.

Transitional Words

American high schools offer elective subjects. **However,** Russian high schools have no electives.

Subordinators

While American high schools offer elective subjects, Russian high schools have a set course of study.

* You may want to review independent and dependent clauses in Appendix C-1, pages 209–220, and the four kinds of connecting words in Chapter 1, pages 18–20.

WORDS TO INDICATE CONTRAST

KEY WORDS	COORDINATORS
unlike	but
different from	yet
despite	

Example	*Example*
Unlike Russian students, American students have a lot of free time.	Many American high school students can wear casual clothes to school, **yet** Russian high school students wear uniforms.
The atmosphere in American classrooms is **different from** the atmosphere in Russian classrooms.	

TRANSITIONAL WORDS	SUBORDINATORS
however	although
nevertheless	even though
in contrast	while
on the other hand	whereas

Example	*Example*
Some American high schools don't offer difficult subjects. **On the other hand,** Russian high schools treat difficult subjects in depth.	**While** some American high schools charge tuition, Russian high schools are free.

WORDS TO INDICATE COMPARISON

KEY WORDS	COORDINATORS
like	and
similar to	
just like	
(be) similar to	
(be) the same as	

Example

Like Muscoda High School, Nashua High School had a strong football team.

The emphasis on football at Muscoda High School was **similar** to the emphasis on that sport at Nashua High School.

Example

Muscoda High School had an excellent band, **and** Nashua High School did, too.

TRANSITIONAL WORDS	SUBORDINATORS
similarly	just as
likewise	
in the same way	

Example

Muscoda High School had an excellent band. **Similarly,** Nashua High School won honors for its band.

Example

Just as Muscoda High School had an excellent band, so did Nashua High School.

ACTIVITY 6-7   Connect the following sentences in four different ways. In your sentences, use the connecting words given. The first one is done as an example.

1. In American schools the chairs can be arranged in a circle. In Russian schools the chairs are in straight rows.

   unlike
   yet
   although
   in contrast

   Unlike American schools, in Russian schools the chairs are in straight rows.
   In American schools the chairs can be arranged in a circle, yet in Russian schools the chairs are in straight rows.
   Although in American schools the chairs can be arranged in a circle, in Russian schools the chairs are in straight rows.
   In American schools the chairs can be arranged in a circle. In contrast, in Russian schools the chairs are in straight rows.

2. In American schools sometimes students eat in class. In Russian schools students do not eat in class.

unlike _____

but _____

whereas _____

on the other hand _____

3. In American schools you can find many male teachers. In Russian schools most of the teachers are women.

different from _____

yet _____

even though _____

however _____

4. In American schools most students are polite. In Russian schools most students are polite.

like _____

and _____

as _____

likewise _____

5. American schools teach basic subjects. Russian schools teach basic subjects.

similar to _____

and _____

just as _____

similarly _____

ACTIVITY 6-8   Read the following paragraph about college students. Then write sentences contrasting high school students with college students. In your sentences, use the connecting words given. The first one is done as an example.

Most students like the freedom they have in college. Usually college students live on their own, in the dormitory or in an apartment. This means they are free to come and go as they like. Their parents can't tell them when to get up, when to go to school, and when to come home. It also means that they are free to wear what they want. There are no parents to comment about their hair styles or their dirty jeans. Finally, they are free to listen to their favorite music without interference from parents.

1. College students usually live on their own.

   unlike   *Unlike college students, high school students usually live with their parents.*

   while   *While college students usually live on their own, high school students usually live with their parents.*

2. College students are free to come and go as they like.

   whereas _____

   different from _____

   on the other hand _____

3. College students are free to wear what they want.

   in contrast _____

   but _____

4. College students can listen to their favorite music.

   although _____

   however _____

ACTIVITY 6-9   Read the following paragraph about college students. Then write sentences showing the similarity between college students and high school students. In your sentences, use the connecting words given. The first one is done as an example.

College students enjoy a variety of extracurricular activities. They can go to large events sponsored by the college, such as football games, concerts, movies, and plays. They also can participate in student organizations. For example, they can run for office in the student government organization, play in the band, or write for the school newspaper. In addition, there are many clubs they can join: the student engineering club, the foreign student association, the Young Republicans, the French club.

1. College students enjoy a variety of extracurricular activities.

   just as   *Just as college students enjoy a variety of extracurricular activities, so do high school students.*

   like   *Like college students, high school students enjoy a variety of extracurricular activities.*

2. College students can go to football games, concerts, movies, and plays.

   similarly _____

   just like _____

3. College students can participate in student organizations.

   in the same way _____

   like _____

   just as_____

4. There are many clubs college students can join.

   likewise _____

   just as _____

   and _____

Grammar Review

The following grammar points will help you write comparison and contrast. If you want to review them, turn to the pages listed below.

Comparative Forms   Page 251
Correlative Conjunctions   Page 254
Run-on Sentences   Page 255
Comma Splices   Page 256

Using the Internet

 INTERNET ACTIVITY   Many colleges and universities have Web sites. Use a search engine such as Google, Yahoo!, or Excite to find two universities you are interested in and do the following.

1. Fill in the following chart. Name the two universities you have chosen. Fill in the points of comparison for Universities A and B from Activity 6-3.

On the Web sites, find information about each university for each point of comparison.

UNIVERSITIES A AND B

UNIVERSITY A	UNIVERSITY B
1. Admission Requirements _____	_____
_____	_____
2. _____	_____
_____	_____
3. _____	_____
_____	_____
4. _____	_____
_____	_____
5. _____	_____
_____	_____
6. _____	_____
_____	_____

2. Compare and contrast the information about the two universities. Which would you rather go to?
3. Explain to a partner or your classmates and teacher which university you would rather go to. Use the information in your points of comparison to support your decision. While speaking, use connecting words to indicate comparison and contrast.
4. When you are finished explaining your reasons, compare your decision with your partner's or classmates'. Do you have similar reasons?
5. Your teacher may ask you to write a paragraph about your decision.

Preparing to Write

Contrasting "Then" and "Now"

The writer often uses comparison and contrast to show how some person, place, or thing has changed over a period of time. For example, if you return to your childhood home, you will often think about how it has changed—how it looked then and how it looks now. This kind of contrast often shows that the thing is better or worse than before.

ACTIVITY 6-10   Read the following paragraphs and answer the questions that follow.

I remember with great joy the orchard surrounding my grandmother's house in Puerto Rico. Her house was a big country house on the top of a little mountain. There was a little dirt road that connected my family's house and the houses of my aunt and uncle to my grandma's house. In the mornings, my cousins and I accompanied my grandma to pick the fruit from the trees around her house. There were many fruit trees—oranges, grapefruit, limes, guava, tamarind, and mango—and we picked the ripe fruit carefully. My favorite tree was a mango tree because sometimes I would sit in its shade and contemplate the view of nature all around me. Also, when we were playing in the orchard, it was a pleasant sensation to feel the humidity of the land and the dew on the leaves with our bare feet. The sounds of the birds got confused with our joyful noise, and as a result formed a harmonic melody heard everyplace on the mountain.

Now the orchard is completely changed. Unlike before, it is now empty and ruined. My granny is gone and her house has been sold. The road that united all the houses has been cut vertically, isolating the houses. The orchard where we picked so many different fruits is almost bare. Many of the trees have been cut down or have died from lack of water. My mango tree was demolished to build a play house. The humidity of the land can no longer be felt; the soil is arid now. When it rains, the water erodes the soil of the mountain, creating ditches and bare places. Even the birds have decreased with time. When once the air was filled with birds' songs, now there is silence. Time has erased my favorite place, but it can never erase my memory of it.

—*Diana I. Robledo*

1. What is the writer's main idea? Write it in a complete sentence. _____

   _____

2. Fill in the following chart. Give the points of comparison that the writer uses. Then list the details that show the change between then and now. The first one is done as an example.

Point of Contrast	Then	Now
dirt road	connected houses	cut
_____	_____	_____
_____	_____	_____
_____	_____	_____
_____	_____	_____

Organizing by Subjects

In the last section, you learned to organize a comparison or contrast paragraph using points of comparison. Another way to organize a comparison or contrast paragraph is according to subjects. With this organizational method, you use the subjects to structure the paragraph and then discuss the points of comparison for each subject. Study the differences between these two ways of organizing comparison and contrast writing.

Organizing by Points
    First Point of Comparison: Attitude
        Subject: Ali
        Subject: Ahmad
    Second Point of Comparison: Teaching Method
        Subject: Ali
        Subject: Ahmad

Organizing by Subjects
    Subject: Ali
        First Point of Comparison: Attitude
        Second Point of Comparison: Teaching Method
    Subject: Ahmad
        First Point of Comparison: Attitude
        Second Point of Comparison: Teaching Method

ACTIVITY 6-11   Reread the paragraphs in Activity 6-10 and answer the following questions.

1. Which method of organization does the writer use?
2. Outline the paragraphs.

Writing

Writing Assignment 2: Comparing and Contrasting

Now you are going to write two paragraphs: a "then" paragraph and a "now" paragraph. In the "then" paragraph, you will show what your topic used to be like. In the "now" paragraph, you will show how it has changed.

1. PREPARE TO WRITE.

   A. First, think of a topic. You may choose one of the topics listed below.

   A Place that You Used to Go to and Have Recently Seen Again

      Examples: a school, a house, a playground, a beach, a market, a store, a barbershop

A Person Who Has Changed

Examples: one of your parents, a sister or brother, your teacher, a friend

Your Attitude Towards a Particular Person Who Has Changed

Your Living Conditions

B. Get ideas about your topic by making a Venn diagram or by brainstorming.

C. Make two lists about the topic. In one list, tell how the subject was in the past. In the other list, tell how it is now.

D. Look over your lists and decide on points of contrast.

E. Decide on a controlling idea.

F. Write an outline for two paragraphs. Organize them by subjects. The first paragraph will tell how the subject was then. The second paragraph will tell how the subject is now.

2. WRITE TWO PARAGRAPHS.

3. REVISE YOUR PARAGRAPHS.

A. Use the Revising Checklist to evaluate your paper, or ask a partner to do it.

B. Revise your paper.

Revising Checklist

1. Do you show how something has changed over time?
2. Do you have a controlling idea? What is it?
3. In the "then" paragraph, do you show how the thing was in the past? Do you give specific details and description?
4. In the "now" paragraph, do you show how the thing has changed?
5. Do you use the same points of contrast in the "now" paragraph as you do in the "then" paragraph?
6. In the "now" paragraph, do you give specific details and description?
7. Do you use appropriate connecting words?
8. Is the paragraph interesting?

More Reading and Writing

Discuss these questions with your classmates or teacher.

1. Look at the posters on page 138.
2. All of them are about the same topic. What is it?
3. What do you think the posters urge people to do?
4. What problems face adults who are illiterate?

Reading

Literacy Around the World

able to read and write

The following accounts were written by three adults who recently became **literate.**° They appeared in various publications and were circulated by UNESCO. As you read them, think about this question: How have these people's lives changed since they became literate?

How Literacy Has Helped Me

Ndugu Rukia Okashi is a 53-year-old farmer living in Arusha, Tanzania. She grows maize, beans, and vegetables, has seven children, and became literate about ten years ago. She says:

There is a great difference in my present situation when compared with the old days. A lot of changes have taken place. When I was required to sign various papers and documents I could only use the thumbprint and I never knew what exactly I was signing. Consequently, I could some-

receive unfair treatment

times **suffer injustices**° and exploitation. Now that I am literate no one can ask me to sign just blindly. I first have to ask what the whole business is all about, I read the papers myself, and it is only after I am satisfied that I agree to sign. If I don't agree with the contents of the documents, I just don't sign. Whereas before one could never refuse to sign a document: you were just asked to put your thumbprint . . . .

Literacy has helped me in many other ways. Through literacy I now know the nutrient values of various foods—those which build the body, those which help us to prevent some diseases, and so on. I know what a balanced diet is.

Formerly, when one walked through the streets one couldn't read any signs. You may come across a "danger" signboard but you continue to walk ahead until someone shouts, "Mama, mama, mama, mama, stop!" But these days, I can read all the signposts such as "Don't pass here, Don't walk on the grass." In traveling also, I used to ask the driver to let me get down at a certain place, but sometimes the driver would take me much further beyond my destination. If such an incident occurs now, I shout and protest.

So now I feel great and self-confident. I have the ability to refuse or disagree, whereas formerly I easily became a victim of great injustices because I was illiterate.

Learning To Read and Write

At the age of thirty, Janice Taylor, of Pembroke, Ontario, Canada, was totally illiterate. She had not continued her studies beyond the fifth year because of adaptation problems, and, unable to read or write, had found herself virtually cut off from normal social life.

One day she heard talk in her neighborhood of ALSO, an organization established to help illiterates.

Since last May, Janice has been the proud possessor of a diploma of the Department of Trade and Technology's Algonquin College and now specializes in the repair of small mechanical and electrical equipment such as typewriters, radios, and light fittings. She says:

At first I found it all very difficult, but I was determined to continue because I wanted to go to college and learn a trade. When you can't read or write, you can't get work, you are poor, you can't take part in many activities, and sometimes you don't even understand what people are saying to you. You are not aware of what is going on around you.

When I started taking the course I was embarrassed about my age and I was afraid that people would laugh at me. I soon found that everybody else felt the same.

Being Reborn

Birke is a 27-year-old woman from Sidamo province, Ethiopia, who has just completed a six-month literacy program. She tells her own story:

The very idea of sending a girl to school was formerly considered immoral in our society. If there was any opportunity at all for education, it was always the boys who were given this privilege. A girl was supposed to stay at home until the day of her marriage. And once married—not to the man of her choice, but to the one who promised the biggest amount of min (dowry)—her chances of going to school became absolutely nonexistent. In fact, in this new phase of her life she had to face many other injustices and hardships. Every day she would have to go to the river to fetch water, collect wood for the fire, and prepare the food; she looked after the cattle and the household, and that was how she would live for the rest of her life.

But times have changed. A small local reading center was set up in our village and those who had already learnt to read would read out to the others what was in the newspapers. When my turn came to attend a literacy class I studied hard and in six months I was able to read and write. Today whenever I get newspapers I enjoy reading them. I have become aware of things. It is like being reborn or like a blind man who has regained his sight. I never thought this would happen in my lifetime.

Comprehension. Answer the following questions.

1. Who is Ndugu Rukia Okashi?
2. After she became literate, what changes took place in her life?
3. How does she feel now?
4. Who is Janice Taylor?
5. How has becoming literate changed her life?
6. Who is Birke?
7. In the past in her society, what could a girl expect in her life?
8. How has life changed in her village?
9. How does she feel about becoming literate?

Discussion. Discuss these questions with your classmates or teacher.

1. Do you find any similarities in the changes in these women's lives? What are they?
2. What feelings do they all share?
3. Do you know anyone who has recently become literate? Tell how that person's life has changed.
4. Is adult illiteracy a problem in your country? If so, how?
5. Does your country have adult literacy programs? Tell about them.

Topics for Discussion and Writing

Your teacher may ask you to discuss or write about one of the following topics.

1. Show how an important event changed your life—getting married, moving to another country, having children, having a close friend with a serious disease.
2. Contrast social attitudes toward dating and marriage in your home country with attitudes in another country.
3. Contrast social attitudes toward dating and marriage held by older and younger people of the same culture.

4. Contrast your attitude as a child toward your parents with your attitude now.
5. Show the similarities between two people that you know well.
6. Show the similarities between the ways two cultures celebrate a holiday, for example, New Year's or Independence Day.
7. Show the similarities or differences between nature in the city and nature in the country.

Chapter **7** Classifying

Theme

The Media

Goals

Writing

To write a paragraph classifying some aspect of the media

To find a principle of classification

To introduce and support categories

To improve cohesion by using connecting words for classification

Reading

To read about and analyze classifications of media

Grammar

To review parallel structure

To review sentence fragments

Getting Started

Journal Writing: My Favorite Kind of Movie

Mass media are the different channels or ways of sending messages to large numbers of people. The media include newspapers, magazines, books, radio, TV, recordings, and movies. For your journal writing, think about movies and answer the following questions:

1. What is your favorite kind of movie? Why?
2. What other kinds of movies are there? List as many kinds as you can think of.

Discussion. Do the following activities.

1. Discuss your favorite kind of movie with your classmates or teacher.
2. Compare your list with your classmates' lists. As a class, make a complete list of types of movies.

CNN® Video Activity: Magazine Wars

 One type of magazine that is very popular in the United States is the kind that has stories about famous people, especially movie and television celebrities. This video describes three magazines that belong to this group.

Before you watch the video, discuss these quesstions with your classmates or teacher.

1. What are the most popular magazines about famous people?
2. Do you enjoy reading those magazines? What kinds of stories do you like the best?
3. Where are popular magazines usually sold?

Understanding the Video

Comprehension. As you watch the video, listen for the following names and terms. After you watch the video, match the names and terms on the left with the explanation on the right by writing the correct letter on the line after each name or term.

1. *People* magazine _____
2. *Us Weekly* _____
3. Julia Roberts _____
4. Mop level _____
5. *Entertainment Weekly* _____

a. Near the floor
b. Nominated for an award for excellence 3 times in 6 years
c. Only 50% of articles about celebrities and entertainment
d. Changed from a monthly to a weekly
e. Appeared on the cover of the first *Us Weekly*

Discussion. After you watch the video, discuss these questions with your classmates or teacher.

1. Why do you think people like to read about movie and television stars and other celebrities?
2. What magazines do you and your classmates enjoy reading? Why?
3. What magazines do you dislike? Why?
4. The magazines described in the video are popular ones for a general audience. What are some types of magazines that are more specialized?

Reading

Discuss these questions with your classmates or teacher.

1. Look at the chart below. What does it show?
2. Can you fill in the empty blanks?
3. Look at the picture of the magazines on page 146. How are the various magazines different from each other?

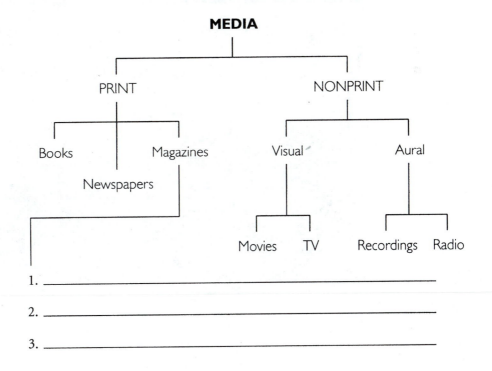

1. _____

2. _____

3. _____

Reading

The Magazine Industry
by Shirley Biagi

This reading is taken from *Media Impact,* a textbook on the media written by Shirley Biagi. Biagi is a professor of mass media at California State University in Sacramento.

predict; foresee
try to please

Sports Illustrated was one of the earliest magazines to **anticipate**° today's trend in magazines. Successful magazines today **cater to**° specialized audiences. You probably have seen a copy of *Sports Illustrated* recently, but you may not have seen *Heavy Duty Trucking, Bassmaster,* or *Inc.* All these publications are ranked among the country's top 400 magazines. They give their readers information that the readers can't find anywhere else, and the number of people who read *Heavy Duty Trucking, Bassmaster,* and *Inc.* might surprise you.

people who receive a magazine regularly

Heavy Duty Trucking, which is more than sixty years old and collects more than $5 million a year from **subscribers**° and advertisers, is ranked third in the country among automotive magazines. Most of the magazine's 95,000 readers own trucks or truck-and-tractor combinations, and they want to know how to make their businesses more profitable.

More than 400,000 people read *Bassmaster,* first published in 1976. Articles tell readers how to find and catch largemouth, smallmouth, and spotted **bass.**° *Bassmaster* collects $8.7 million a year.

a kind of fish
person who starts and manages a business

The typical *Inc.* reader is an **entrepreneur**° with a small- to medium-size business. The magazine began publishing in 1979. More than half a million people read *Inc.* every month, and it averages 125 pages of advertising in each issue. Advertisers and subscribers spend $44 million a year on *Inc.*

***

Magazines usually are divided into three types: (1) consumer publications; (2) trade, technical, and professional publications; and (3) company publications.

You probably are most familiar with consumer magazines, which are popularly marketed: *Time, Vogue, Esquire, Bassmaster,* and *Inc.,* for example. In the magazine business, "consumer" magazines are not just those that give buying advice. This term refers to all magazines sold by subscription or at newsstands, supermarkets, and bookstores. As a group, consumer magazines make the most money because they have the most readers and carry the most advertising.

Trade, technical, and professional magazines are read by people in a particular industry to learn more about their business. *Heavy Duty Trucking* is a trade magazine. So are the *Columbia Journalism Review* (published by Columbia University) and *American Medical News* (published by the American Medical Association). These magazines are issued by private companies for their subscribers (such as *Heavy Duty Trucking*); [by] universities or university-connected organizations for their subscribers (such as the *Columbia Journalism Review*); or by professional associations for their members (such as *American Medical News*). Most trade, technical, and professional magazines carry advertising directed at the professions they serve.

Company magazines are produced by businesses for their employees and **stockholders.**° These magazines usually don't carry advertising. Their main purpose is to promote the company. Du Pont, for instance, publishes a company magazine called *Du Pont Context.*

people who own part of a company

Comprehension. Answer the following questions.

1. What is the trend in today's magazines?
2. What are some examples of specialized magazines?
3. Who do these magazines appeal to?
4. What are consumer magazines?
5. What kind of advertising appears in consumer magazines? Give some examples.
6. What are trade, technical, and professional magazines?
7. Who publishes trade, technical, and professional magazines?
8. What kind of advertising appears in trade, technical, and professional magazines? Give some examples.
9. What are company magazines?
10. How are company magazines different from the other two kinds of magazines?

Discussion. Discuss these questions with your classmates or teacher.

1. What kind of magazines do you like to read? Why?
2. Bring a magazine to class or think of one you are familiar with. Tell the following about it.
   a. What kind is it? (Refer to the three types listed in the reading.)
   b. What kind of information can you get in it?
   c. What kind of advertising does it have?

NOTE: If you want to read another essay giving a classification, read "Types of Newspapers in Ivory Coast" by Ledja Sylvie Amon on pages 167–169.

Preparing to Write

Finding a Principle of Classification

One way to analyze is to put things into groups. Putting things into groups allows the writer to divide a large topic into smaller parts. For example, in the reading, Biagi divides the topic "magazines" into three groups. This makes the topic easier to write about and helps her readers understand it better. This kind of analysis is called **classification.**

Classification is common in all kinds of academic and professional writing. Geologists classify rocks, computer scientists sort bits of information, and businesspeople categorize consumers.

When a writer divides a topic into groups, he or she does so according to a guideline or reason. For example, Biagi groups magazines according to specialized audiences: consumers, trades/professions, and companies. The reason or guideline used to make the grouping is called a **principle of classification.**

Imagine that you want to write a paragraph about the students in your class. It would be difficult to write about each student in a logical way. It would be easier to write about them if you put them in groups of students sharing similar characteristics. You could use level of education as your principle of classification. In this case you would have two groups: graduate and undergraduate.

What are some other ways to classify the students in your class? Fill in the blanks below:

Students can be classified:
according to   their nationality.
according to   _____.
according to   _____.
according to   _____.

When a writer classifies, he or she uses only one principle of classification. For example, if you are classifying the students in your class, you could classify them according to their majors or according to their attitude about the class. However, you could not divide students into biology majors, engineering majors, and lazy students.

ACTIVITY 7-1   The topics below have been divided into several categories. Read the topics and categories. Give the principle of classification that has been used to make the categories. The first one is done as an example.

1. Topic: Print media: books, newspapers, magazines
                   Principle of classification: <u>physical form of media</u>

2. Topic: Newspapers: daily, weekly
                   Principle of classification: _____

3. Topic: Newspapers: well-written, average, badly written
                   Principle of classification: _____

4. Topic: Books: fiction, nonfiction
                   Principle of classification: _____

5. Topic: Textbooks: inexpensive, average, expensive
                   Principle of classification: _____

6. Topic: Consumer magazines: children, adults
                   Principle of classification: _____

ACTIVITY 7-2   Look at the clustering diagrams that follow. Each one divides a group into several categories. Determine the principle of classification that is used. Find the category that does not belong.

1.

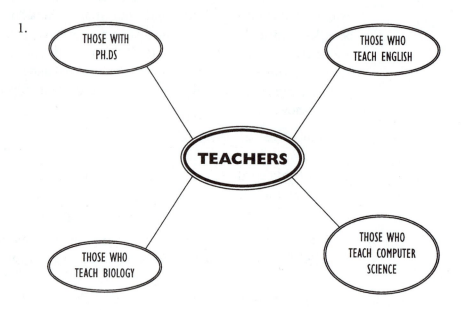

2.

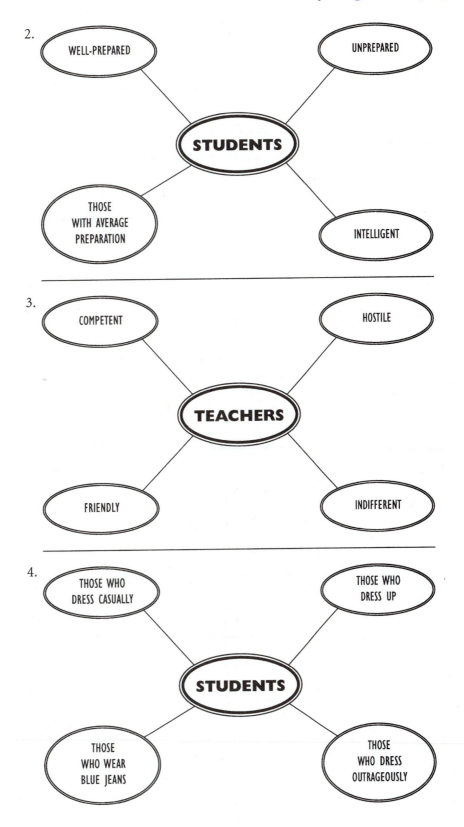

3.

4.

ACTIVITY 7-3   Look at each topic and category given below. Determine the principle of classification. Then, write at least two more categories that belong in that classification.

1. Topic: Movies

    Principle of classification: _____

    Categories: *those with a lot of violence* _____

    _____

    _____

    _____

    _____

2. Topic: TV programs

    Principle of classification: _____

    Categories: *those that educate* _____

    _____

    _____

    _____

    _____

3. Topic: TV news programs

    Principle of classification: _____

    daily news _____

    _____

    _____

    _____

    _____

4. Topic: Newscasters

    Principle of classification: _____

    Those who are friendly _____

    _____

    _____

_____

_____

5. Topic: TV sitcoms

   Principle of classification: _____

   Those produced in the 1970s _____

   _____

   _____

   _____

   _____

6. Topic: Radio talk show hosts

   Principle of classification: _____

   outrageous _____

   _____

   _____

   _____

   _____

7. Topic: Rock musicians

   Principle of classification: _____

   known worldwide _____

   _____

   _____

   _____

   _____

8. Topic: Radio stations

   Principle of classification: _____

   those that play only music _____

   _____

   _____

ACTIVITY 7-4   Look at the TV channel chart given below. It lists some of the networks available on cable TV in New Orleans. Read the descriptions of the channels. Sort them into groups according to a principle of classification.

Channel #	NETWORK • Programming
2* (U/PiN)	WUPL (2) UPN
3*	WWL (4) CBS
4* PREVUE	PREVUE CHANNEL
5# HBO	HOME BOX OFFICE Blockbuster movies, specials, sports and family programs. HBO
6*	GOVERNMENT ACCESS (J.P./ST.C) NOETC (N.O.)
7*	WDSU (6) NBC
8*	EDUCATIONAL ACCESS (J.P./ST.C) GOVERNMENT ACCESS (N.O.)
9* FOX	WVUE (8) FOX
10* COX METRO TELEVISION	
11* abc	WGNO (26) ABC
12* PBS	WYES (12) PBS
13* WNOL (38)	IND
14* PBS	WLAE (32) PBS
15* WWL-TV's NewsWatch	Local News Around the Clock
16# SHOWTIME	SHOWTIME Exclusive movies, original series, family shows. SHO
17* SuperStation TBS	TURNER BROADCASTING SYSTEM Atlanta-Airs the best in specials, movies and sports. TBS
18* WGN	WGN An independent station from Chicago, Illinois. WGN
19* TLC	THE LEARNING CHANNEL Engaging programs about science, history and world cultures. TLC
20# cinemax	CINEMAX Over 170 movies per month—with a different kind of movie every day of the week. MAX
21* QVC NETWORK	QVC NETWORK A home shopping service allowing subscribers to order name brand merchandise via TV. QVC
22* BET	BLACK ENTERTAINMENT TELEVISION America's pioneer in showcasing Black Entertainment BET
23 A&E	A&E NETWORK An entertainment network featuring original biographies, mysteries and specials. A&E
24	THE WEATHER CHANNEL Live 24-hour broadcast of national and local weather. TWC
25 TNT	TURNER NETWORK TELEVISION Featuring the finest motion pictures, made-for-cable movies, sports, sitcoms, dramatic series and more. TNT
26 AMC	AMERICAN MOVIE CLASSICS The greatest films of Hollywood's Golden Years. AMC
27 MTV	MTV: MUSIC TELEVISION 24-hour video music channel in stereo, reflecting the spirit of rock 'n' roll. MTV

CHANNEL CHART

Introducing the Categories

The topic sentence for a classification paragraph should give the topic and the principle of classification. Look at this example:

Children's TV programs can be classified according to their purpose.

Here the topic is *children's TV programs* and the principle of classification is *their purpose.*

Notice the verb that is used in the example above. What is it? There are a number of other verbs that indicate classification and thus are useful in topic sentences. They include the following: *classify, group, categorize, divide, sort, organize.* A classification paragraph also has sentences to identify each category. Look at these examples:

The first category consists of programs that are designed to teach.
The next group includes programs that entertain.
The last category is made up of programs that both teach and entertain.

ACTIVITY 7-5   Choose one of the topics listed in Activity 7-3 and do the following.

1. Write a topic sentence that gives your topic and principle of classification.

_____

_____

2. Write a sentence to introduce each of the categories.

_____

_____

_____

_____

_____

Sometimes the topic sentence contains only the topic for classification and the categories. Look at this example:

Children's TV programs can be classified into three categories: those that teach, those that entertain, and those that do both.

What is the topic?

What are the three categories?

What is the principle of classification? Is it given in the sentence?

Even if the principle of classification is not given in the topic sentence, it must be clear in the writer's mind.

To introduce the categories in this way, the writer uses two things:

a colon

parallel structure

Parallel structure means using the same grammatical form for all the classes. (You may want to review parallel structure in the Grammar Review C-7 pages 259–260.) Typically, clauses, adjectives, nouns, or adverbs are used in parallel structure. Look at the different structures below:

Clauses   Newspapers can be classified according to frequency of publication: those that are published daily and those that are published weekly.

Adjectives   There are only two kinds of moviegoers: polite and obnoxious.

Nouns   Magazines usually are divided into three types: consumer publications, trade publications, and company publications.

Adverbs   Most people respond to TV talk shows in one of three ways: eagerly, indifferently, or reluctantly.

All of the above topic sentences use parallel structure.

Useful nouns for introducing categories include these: *sorts, divisions, categories, classes, kinds, types, groups, aspects, qualities, characteristics.*

ACTIVITY 7-6   Choose four of the topics listed in Activity 7-3. For each one, write a sentence to introduce the categories. Use a colon and parallel grammatical structure. Use a different structure for each one (clauses, nouns, adjectives, adverbs).

Example: Movies can be classified into three groups: those with no violence, those with a moderate amount of violence, and those with a lot of violence.

1. _____

_____

2. _____

_____

3. _____

_____

4. _____

_____

Supporting the Categories

After the writer has decided on the principle of classification and categories, he or she must think about support for the categories. Here are guidelines for you to follow to develop support for the categories. For each category, you need to do the following:

1. Define or describe the group. What are the common characteristics of the members of the group?
2. Give examples of typical members of the group.
3. For second or third categories, you need to show how this group is different from the other group or groups. How does group one differ from group two?

ACTIVITY 7-7   Read the following paragraph and answer the questions that follow.

Types of Newspapers in India

Newspapers in India are classified into two categories according to the amount and completeness of information in them. Newspapers in the first category have more information and truth. Those in the second category do not have much information and sometimes they hide the truth. Newspapers in the first category have news collected from different parts of the country and also from different countries. They also have a lot of sports and business news and classified ads. The information they give is clear and complete and it is supported by showing pictures. The best known example of this category is the *Indian Express*. Important news goes on the first page with big headlines, photographs from different angles, and complete information. For example, in 1989–90, the Indian prime minister, Rajive Ghandi, was killed by a terrorist using a bomb. This newspaper investigated the situation and gave information that helped the CBI to get more support. They also showed diagrams of the area where the prime minister was killed and the positions of the bodies after the attack. This helped the reader understand what happened. This newspaper gave a lot of information on this case, right up to the end. Unlike newspapers in the first category, newspapers in the second category do not give as much information. They do not have international news, sports, or business news and they do not have classified ads. Also, the news they give is not complete. For example, the newspaper *Hindi* gave news on the death of the prime minister, but the news was not complete. The newspaper didn't investigate the terrorist group or try to find out why this happened. Also, it did not show any pictures from the attack or give any news the next day. It just gave the news when it happened, but it didn't follow up. Therefore, newspapers in the first group are more popular than those in the second group.

—*Purnachander Thangada*

1. Underline the topic sentence. What is the principle of classification the writer uses?
2. What are the categories the topic is divided into?
3. What are the characteristics of the members of the first group? The second group?
4. What examples does the writer give?
5. Does the writer show how the second group is different from the first group?

ACTIVITY 7-8   Using one of the topics you worked on in Activity 7-5 or 7-6, do the following for each category:

1. Write several sentences that give the general characteristics of the group.
2. List examples you could use.
3. Write several sentences that show how the second group is different from the first group.

ACTIVITY 7-9   Write the paragraph you prepared in Activity 7-8.

Using Language Effectively

Cohesion: Connecting Words for Classification

In writing a classification paragraph, you will use several types of connecting words. Some of them are listed on page 159 and 160.

WORDS TO INTRODUCE CATEGORIES

KEY WORDS*	TRANSITIONAL WORDS
NOUNS	
the first group	in addition
the next category	finally
one type	
another kind	
the second division	

Examples

The first category consists of newspapers that are published daily.

One type of magazine is the consumer magazine.

Example

In addition, there is the type that is the least popular: the boring teachers.

VERBS

We can classify

  group

  categorize

Something can be divided

    sorted

    organized

Examples

We can **classify** magazines into three groups.

Magazines can **be divided** into three groups.

WORDS TO CONTRAST CATEGORIES

KEY WORDS	SUBORDINATORS
unlike	whereas
different from	while
in contrast to	

* Verbs and nouns to introduce categories are discussed on pages 155–156.

Examples	*Examples*
Unlike consumer magazines, company magazines do not have advertising.	**Whereas** consumer magazines have advertising, company magazines do not.
In contrast to movies in the first group, movies in the second group are more serious.	**While** movies in the first group are not very serious, those in the second group are.

WORDS TO INTRODUCE EXAMPLES

KEY WORDS

a good example

one example

is typical of

Examples

A good example of a consumer magazine is *Bassmaster.*

Heavy Duty Trucking **is typical of** a trade magazine.

ACTIVITY 7-10   Read the following paragraph, which does not have key words. Rewrite it, using key words from the chart above.

Example: As a regular moviegoer, I have noticed that people have different attitudes about talking when they go to the movies. Moviegoers can be classified **into two groups** according to the way they talk. **The first group consists of . . .**

As a regular moviegoer, I have noticed that people have different attitudes about talking when they go to the movies. Moviegoers can be classified according to the way they talk. Some people talk normally. When they come into the theater with someone, they talk quietly until the movie starts. Once the movie starts, they don't make comments to each other or talk out loud. Some people talk a lot. When they come into the theater, they talk and laugh out loud. Once they find their seats, they continue to talk. They hardly notice when the movie starts because they are still talking and laughing. Even though people in the other group give them dirty looks, the people in this group talk and laugh throughout the movie. Sometimes they repeat what the actors are saying and sometimes they ask each other about what was said. Because they are so noisy, they can't hear what is going on in the movie and, unfortunately, neither can the people sitting near them. People in this group are inconsiderate of the needs of others.

Cohesion: Repetition of Key Ideas

There are a number of ways to improve the smooth flow, or cohesion, of paragraphs. The writer can depend on connecting words, which have been listed in each chapter, and pronoun consistency, which was studied in Chapter 4. Another method the writer can use is repeating the key ideas in a paragraph. **Key words** are the important words in the topic sentence. Repeating them or using synonyms for them improves cohesion.

Read the following paragraph, in which the key ideas are underlined.

Many people turn on the radio to listen to music. But what station do they turn to? People who listen to rock music typically have three choices: stations that play new rock, stations that play classic rock, and stations that offer a blend of new and old. In the first group are stations that typically play the newest hits by the hottest groups. These stations constantly popularize new albums by new bands. For example, KHOM in New Orleans recently featured two new groups and their latest songs: "Butterfly" by Crazytown and "Survivor" by Destiny's Child. These rock music stations usually appeal to young people, aged 18–24, who want to know the latest in rock music. In the second category are stations that play classic rock. These stations may focus on music from a particular era such as the 80s or present a blend of old favorites, mixing songs from the 60s, 70s, 80s, and 90s. For example, in New Orleans on WRNO, you might hear a Beatles tune, "Strawberry Fields," from the 60s or an Eagles hit, "Hotel California," from the 70s. These stations typically appeal to older listeners, those in the 25–40 age group, who want to hear the rock music that was popular when they were young. Radio stations in the third category cover all of rock music, mixing the latest hits with some golden oldies. On these stations you might first hear "Love Don't Cost a Thing," a current song by Jennifer Lopez, and then "The Waiting," a Tom Petty hit from twenty-five years ago. These stations appeal to people of all ages, but especially to people who want to be familiar with the entire field. Thus, rock music

<u>radio stations</u> offer listeners a number of options; which people choose usually depends upon their age and taste.

The key words are the following:

radio
music
station
rock

Notice how the key words help to give the paragraph cohesion. Instead of repeating the key words again and again, the writer may use synonyms for them. For example, in the paragraph above, instead of repeating the word *music*, the writer uses the word *hits* to mean the same thing. Reread the paragraph and find other synonyms for the word *music*.

ACTIVITY 7-11   Read the paragraphs below and do the following.

1. In the first paragraph, underline the key ideas that give the paragraph cohesion.
2. In the second paragraph, fill in the key ideas that have been left out.

Magazines aimed at women have been around for a long time. Now, with so many women working outside the home, you would think that some modern women's magazines would focus on women at work. However, a survey of the newsstand shows that this is not the case. Now, as in the past, publications for women try to attract readers by focusing on women's traditional concerns: beauty and homemaking. In fact, women's magazines can be divided into two groups based on content: those focused on fashion and beauty and those focused on homemaking and raising children. Magazines in the first group attract women readers by presenting articles about appearance. Publications in this group include *Glamour, Cosmopolitan,* and *Mademoiselle.* They typically have articles that describe the latest clothing styles or tell how to put on makeup. The latest issue of *Glamour,* for example, had an article entitled "Clothes To Flirt In" and a column on how to straighten hair. These magazines also have advice columns on dating and love relationships, articles on health and fitness, and reports on movie stars or popular singers. The pages of these periodicals are filled with beautiful women dressed in elegant evening gowns, sexy jeans, and fashionable shoes. They are designed to appeal to women's concerns about their appearance.

Magazines in the second group focus on homemaking and _____. This group includes _____ like *Ladies' Home Journal, Family Circle,* and *Good Housekeeping.* The last issue of *Good Housekeeping,* for example, had twenty-five Christmas cookie recipes, a column on how to make Christmas tree ornaments, an article entitled "Teaching Kids the Joy of Generosity," and several stories dealing with health ("Health Check" and "The Secrets of People Who Never Get Sick"). Unlike the magazines in the first group, which focus on women's looks, these _____ focus on _____ role in the home. While beauty and homemaking are two areas of concern for women, many _____ work outside the home. It is surprising that there are no magazines focused on _____ lives at work.

ACTIVITY 7-12   Read the paragraph you wrote in Activity 7-9 and do the following.

1. Underline the key ideas that give the paragraph cohesion.
2. Can you improve cohesion by adding key words in any sentences?
3. Do you use synonyms for the key words in any sentences? If not, with the help of a partner or your teacher, find synonyms for the key words.
4. Rewrite the paragraph using key words and synonyms.

Grammar Review

The following grammar points will help you write paragraphs of classification. If you want to review them, turn to the pages listed below.

Parallel Structure   Page 259
Sentence Fragments   Page 260

Using the Internet

INTERNET ACTIVITY   We can divide Internet addresses into groups based on a principle of classification. Many Internet addresses end in one of these abbreviations:

.gov
.edu
.com

1. What is the principle of classification for these groups? Write it here.

_____

_____

2. Using a search engine such as Google, Yahoo!, or Excite, go to several Web sites in the groups listed in the chart below. What kind of information do you find on these Web sites? Fill in the chart.

INFORMATION

GROUP	DESCRIPTION OF GROUP	WEB SITES YOU VISITED	KIND OF INFORMATION ON SITES
.gov			
.edu			
.com			

3. Using your chart, explain your classification of Internet addresses to a partner or your classmates and teacher. Give the principle of classification, a description of each group, examples of each group (the Web sites you visited), and the kind of information the Web sites provide. While speaking, use connecting words for classification.

4. Compare your chart with your partner's or classmates'. What differences do you find?

5. Your teacher may ask you to write a paragraph explaining your classification of Internet addresses.

Writing

Writing Assignment: Classifying

Now you are going to write a paragraph classifying some aspect of the media. (You can choose another topic if your teacher agrees.)

1. PREPARE TO WRITE.
   A. First, think about a topic. Following are some examples. You might think of others.

   A Major Media Group:

       Types of books, newspapers, magazines

       Types of radio programs, TV programs, movies, recordings

   A Smaller Media Group:

       Types of novels, fashion magazines, sports magazines

       Children's TV programs, police dramas, how-to shows

       Types of People in the Media:

       Writers, radio DJs, talk show hosts, singers, actors, movie directors, newscasters

   Other Topics

       People—types of teachers, students, bus drivers

       Buildings—hotels, stadiums

       Vacations

       Leisure-time activities

   B. To get ideas about your topic, use one of the methods in Appendix B. You may want to do clustering or to brainstorm a list of ideas about your topic.

C. Look over your notes and decide on a principle of classification. Write out the principle.

D. Decide on the categories.

E. Decide on support for your categories.

F. Write an outline.

2. WRITE THE PARAGRAPH.

3. REVISE THE PARAGRAPH.

A. Ask a partner to evaluate your paragraph using the Paragraph Guidelines, or do it yourself using the Revising Checklist.

B. Revise your paragraph.

Paragraph Guidelines

1. Write out the topic sentence.
2. Circle the topic the writer is classifying.
3. Underline the principle of classification.
4. List the categories.
5. Is there a single principle of classification?
6. Does the writer describe and define each group?
7. Are there examples for each group?
8. Are there appropriate connecting words to introduce the categories, to contrast categories, and to give examples?
9. Does the writer repeat key words and use synonyms?
10. What part of the paragraph did you enjoy the most?
11. What part would you like to know more about?

Revising Checklist

1. Do you divide the topic into groups?
2. Do you have a single, clear principle of classification? What is it?
3. Are the categories distinct and clear?
4. Do you give enough support for each group? Do you define and describe each group?
5. Do you give examples of typical members for each group?
6. Do you show the differences between groups?
7. Do you use appropriate connecting words to introduce the groups, to contrast groups, and to introduce examples?
8. Do you repeat key words and phrases?

More Reading and Writing

Types of Newspapers in Ivory Coast
by Ledja Sylvie Amon

This essay was written in 1991 by Ledja Sylvie Amon, when she was a student at the University of Côte d'Ivoire (Ivory Coast) in Abidjan, West Africa.

Since the coming of a multi-party political system to Côte d'Ivoire, we have noticed a proliferation of newspapers compared with those that existed formerly, as if people had been prevented from expressing themselves for a long time. The multi-party system is an opportunity for people to put their opinions about the social, political, and economic life of their country into words. On the whole, newspapers in Côte d'Ivoire can be classified into two main groups according to their political **affiliation:**° on the one hand, the pro-government newspapers, and, on the other hand, newspapers of the opposition. The newspapers of both categories are printed in Abidjan, but this does not prevent them from having different accounts of the same events.

connection; association

Unlike the newspapers of the opposition, the pro-government ones always support and encourage the government's actions. Their purpose is to select events to write about and publish according to their political affiliation and interests. The pro-government papers publish stories which are not **prejudicial to**° the government's interests. Before publishing the news, there is a committee composed of people in the Department of Communication whose role it is to check and control the news. The journalist never sees his own ideas printed on the page. What he sees and writes about during his reporting is changed by the committee in order to be adjusted to the government's policy. A story which, once published, would urge people to rebel is simply hidden. The problem with this kind of newspaper is that it hides the truth; the events are not objectively analyzed. The journalist does not work as a journalist but rather as a news reader.

against; not in favor of

The best known of the government-owned newspapers is the daily *Fraternité Matin,* which, in addition to general news and national and international events, focuses on political events. It informs the reader

group

of the government's good actions and policy of development in different areas of the country. For example, if there is a meeting between the president and foreign heads of state or a **delegation**° of American businessmen, it informs the reader about the reasons for these visits, including the benefit of their actions: the firm they plan to create that will help our country transform raw materials into manufactured goods. In addition to political events, which are its strength, it contains a large variety of items ranging from deaths, weddings, and horoscopes to entertainment such as sports, games, and TV programs.

fair, impartial

The newspapers of the opposition, such as *Nouvelle Horizon, La Tribune du Banco,* and *Liberté,* are characterized by their **objective**° analyses. They aim to lead the people to sudden awareness. The people must be free to express themselves about the political life of their country. They must also be free to approve or denounce any government action. Thus, these newspapers are dominated by politics. They inform the reader about the way the country is ruled by politicians, and they criticize anyone, even the president. The main characteristic of these newspapers is their objectivity because their journalists' own views and analysis of events are not controlled in order to select information to print. They can publish their views on events without any restriction. Their target is the government and its action. Friday, the seventeenth of May, when the commandos of Daloa came by night to repress students, the government tried to hide the truth by saying that the students, after having destroyed public property, were caught for identity control and released afterwards.* But the newspapers of the opposition revealed the truth about this action. They showed photographs of the wounded, collected evidence, and published it. They blamed the government for that action and asked the government to resign. Because of these qualities, the opposition newspapers appeal to a great number of readers. The headlines arouse their curiosity, because they are not accustomed to reading a paper criticizing the actions of the government. They also appeal to readers looking for justice and liberty.

It is obvious to me that the two categories are clearly opposed. The first category, by hiding the truth, protects the government's own interest, trying not to **tarnish its public image.**° The second category expresses the facts and through its objective analysis brings out the truth of

make itself look bad

---

* The writer is referring to a particular incident in which the government used military force against university students. After the military (commandos of Daloa) broke up a student demonstration, the students burned a government building (public property). The military then went to the student dormitory at night and arrested some of the students (caught for identity control and released afterwards). The students accused the soldiers of brutality and murder.

events. If only this conflict could be stopped, and all the newspapers were independent and not affiliated with any political parties, if they would not act in any government's favor, they would not only be objective but would contain enriched debates which would school the citizen and develop his critical mind.

Comprehension. Answer the following questions.

1. What is the topic and principle of classification?
2. What are the two categories?
3. Why has there been an increase in newspapers in Côte d'Ivoire?
4. How does the writer describe or define the first group?
5. What examples does the writer give of newspapers in the first group?
6. How does the writer describe or define the second group?
7. What examples does the writer give of newspapers in the second group?
8. What is the writer's attitude about the two kinds of newspapers? How do you know?

Topics for Discussion and Writing

Your teacher may ask you to discuss or write about one of the following topics.

1. Classify one kind of media according to political affiliation.
2. Classify famous people according to political affiliation or use another principle of classification.
3. Classify your friends according to political affiliation (Do you have some friends who are conservative and some who are liberal?) or use another principle of classification.
4. Classify parties or holidays.
5. Advertising is used to support the media. Classify TV or radio advertisements.
6. Bring a magazine to class. Look at all of the ads in the magazine and classify them.
7. Go to a newsstand and do a survey of men's magazines or another kind of magazine. Then classify them.

Chapter 8 Evaluating Effects

Theme
Technology

Goals

Writing

To write an essay evaluating the effects of an invention

To expand a paragraph into an essay

To understand the parts of an essay

To outline an essay

To improve cohesion by using cohesion words to connect paragraphs

Reading

To read about and evaluate the effects of technology

Grammar

To review adverbial clauses of result

To review reduced adverbial clauses

Getting Started

Journal Writing: The Effects of an Invention

Technology has brought many inventions and innovations into our lives. Some examples are computers, VCRs, telephone answering machines, organ transplants, and artificial sweeteners. Can you think of some more examples?

These inventions have many effects on our lives. Some of the effects are negative and some are positive. Choose an invention or innovation to write about in your journal. Answer the following questions.

1. What is the invention?
2. What is your experience with this invention?
3. What are some advantages of this invention?
4. What are some disadvantages of this invention?
5. Do the advantages outweigh the disadvantages or vice versa?

Discussion. Explain the advantages and disadvantages of this invention to your teacher or classmates.

CNN® Video Activity: On-Line Privacy

One popular feature of computers is the ability to send and receive electronic mail. This video explains, however, that our e-mail messages are not always private—even after we delete them. Before you watch the video, discuss these questions with your classmates or teacher.

1. How have computers made our lives easier?
2. How have computers made our lives harder?
3. What are some advantages and disadvantages of e-mail?

Understanding the Video

Comprehension. Read the following questions. As you watch the video, take brief notes. After you watch the video, answer the questions.

1. Do e-mail messages disappear from a computer's hard drive when they are deleted?
2. Is it easy to recover deleted e-mail?
3. What are "shredder programs"? Do they work?
4. What is the only way to make sure the deleted files on a computer are never recovered?

Discussion. After you watch the video, discuss these questions with your classmates or teacher.

1. Which kinds of messages should be sent by e-mail, and which should not be sent?
2. Do computers make it difficult for people to keep their lives private? If so, in what ways?
3. Do the advantages of e-mail outweigh its disadvantages?
4. How may times a day do you use a computer at home, school, or work.

Reading

Discuss these questions with your classmates or teacher.

1. Look at the photographs below and on page 173. For each one, answer these questions:
   a. What invention is being used in this picture?
   b. What are some of the uses of this invention?
   c. What are some of its advantages?
   d. What are some of its disadvantages?

Reading

Privacy and the Computer
by Edward F. Dolan

This reading is taken from a chapter in a book entitled *Your Privacy: Protecting It in a Nosy World.* It was written by Edward F. Dolan, a writer of nonfiction books for young people and adults.

There was a time when any personal information that was gathered about us—from our name and address on a job application to the grades we earned in school—was typed on a piece of paper and tucked away in a file cabinet, there to join other pieces of paper about us. It could remain there for years and, often forgotten, never reach the outside world.

Things have **done a complete about-face**° since then. Responsible for the change has been the astonishingly swift development in recent years of that "super electronic device of the century"—the computer. Today, any data that is collected about us in one place or another—and for one reason or another—can be stored in a computer bank. It can then be easily passed to other computer banks—banks of all sizes that are now to be found throughout the nation. They are owned by individuals and by private businesses and corporations, lending institutions, direct mailing and telemarketing firms, credit bureaus, credit card companies, charitable and religious organizations, and government agencies at the local, state, and federal level.

A growing number of Americans are seeing the **accumulation**° and distribution of computerized data as a frightening invasion of their privacy. Surveys show that the number of worried Americans has been steadily growing through recent years as the computer becomes increasingly efficient, easier to operate, and less costly to purchase and maintain. In 1970, a national survey showed that 37 percent of the people questioned felt their privacy was being invaded. Seven years later, 47 percent expressed the same worry. A 1990 survey, which was conducted by one of the country's largest credit bureaus, revealed that the number of alarmed citizens had shot up to 76 percent.

Aside from the massive amount of material that is involved, the use of the computer for the storage of personal data is widely **condemned**° on a number of counts. The information can easily get into the hands of individuals and organizations that have neither a right nor a reason to use it.

---

changed completely; been reversed

gathering; collection

considered bad

negative
comments

The **criticisms**° include the charge that it is all too easy to store out-of-date personal information in the computer—information that can be damaging to the subject. Here is a case in point. In 1977, a young salesman was turned down for the post of sales manager with a Midwestern company because of an entry that had been made in his employment record five years earlier while he was working for a department store. The entry went into his record after he had been photographed taking part in a demonstration against the Vietnam War and branded him a **"radical,"**° a term that, in the minds of many, automatically means a "troublemaker."

extreme, perhaps
violent, person

cautious; careful

Today, the man says, "I opposed the U.S. involvement in Vietnam, just as many other perfectly loyal Americans did. I was in college at the time and a lot of students were demonstrating against the war. By the time I applied for the sales manager job, I was long gone from college. I was married and had a family. I had become **conservative**° in my political views. The term radical just didn't apply to me anymore—if it ever did in the first place. But it still lost me a job."

a company con-
trolled by another
company
a series of unpaid
bills

Another major criticism holds that mistaken data is allowed to get into the computer banks. Consider what happened some years ago to a retired speech writer in Virginia. As reported in a November issue of *Time* magazine, he was bewildered when a local bank rejected his request for a loan. He then learned that a **subsidiary**° of a national credit bureau had been merging his credit history with that of a man with the same name—but a man who had a **string of bad debts.**° The writer spent weeks working on the mix-up with the credit bureau and thought that he had finally cleared up the matter—only to be turned down for a loan in 1990, at which time he found that his file had again been invaded with information about the man with the same name.

search in a
disorganized way

false; dishonest

The people who operate and maintain computer banks like to insist that the material in their banks is safe from invasion by outsiders. But the truth of the matter is that the banks can be invaded and their data removed. Many of the invasions have been for criminal purposes. Jeffrey Rothfeder, in *Privacy for Sale,* proves the point with a startling example. He writes of gangs that come to the United States from certain countries. On arriving here, they seek jobs as security guards. The jobs are low-paying and are easy to land because employers find them hard to fill. On being assigned to commercial buildings at night, the members **rummage through**° file cabinets, desks, and the office computers to pick up personal employee data that ranges from names, addresses, and Social Security numbers to job titles and earnings. . . . They then use the data to obtain credit cards with **phony**° applications. With the cards, they purchase merchandise worth thousands of dollars and rent expensive cars. Then, before the innocent victims or the authorities know what has

large

happened, the gangs ship everything back to their countries, there to be sold for a **hefty°** profit. Rothfeder adds that, according to a memo by one of the country's leading credit bureaus, the gangs pull off as many as 100,000 deals each year.

Comprehension. Answer the following questions.

1. What is the main idea of paragraphs one and two?
2. What kinds of organizations can get personal information about us?
3. What is the main idea of paragraph three?
4. What kind of support does the writer give for the main idea in paragraph three?
5. What is the first criticism against storing personal data in computer banks?
6. What is the support for the first criticism?
7. What is the second criticism against storing personal data in computer banks?
8. How is the second criticism supported?
9. What is the last criticism against storing personal data in computer banks?
10. How is the last criticism supported?
11. Write about five sentences summarizing the reading for someone who has not read it.

Discussion. Discuss these questions with your classmates or teacher.

1. Do you think computers invade our privacy? Why or why not?
2. Do you think computers have more advantages than disadvantages or more disadvantages than advantages?
3. Have you had an experience in which your privacy was invaded by a computer? Tell what happened.

NOTE: If you want to read about the advantages of technology, read the following:

"Kid Finder" by Suzanne Kantra Kirschner on pages 195–197.
"High-Tech Relic Hunting" by Michael Carroll on page 199.

Preparing to Write

Evaluating Effects

To evaluate is to determine the value or worth of something. When we evaluate, we use words like *good, bad, better, worse, benefits, advantages, disadvantages*. These words indicate a value judgement; they give the writer's opinion. In the chapters of this book, for example, you have been evaluating your writing to see if it is good.

We often evaluate the **effects** of an action or item. We evaluate effects in university courses, at work, and in our private lives. Technology has provided us with many inventions and innovations that have affected our lives. If we want to evaluate the effects of these inventions, we first must determine what the effects, or results, of these inventions are, and then we can evaluate their benefits.

To determine the effects of something, we often ask the question **what.** For example, we might ask these questions:

What are the effects of fax machines on small businesses?
What are the effects of computers in education?
What are the effects of television on the elderly?
What are the effects of organ transplants?
What are the effects of cell phones on teenagers?

ACTIVITY 8-1   Choose one of the questions given above or think of another invention to write about. List as many effects as you can think of. Here is an example:

Topic: What are the effects of computers on the banking industry?

Transactions at banks are fast and easy
      teller can call up your account, complete transaction,
      and computer gives printout

Transactions at banks are convenient
      can move bank account from one branch to another
      without paperwork

ATM machines are fast, easy, and convenient
      can use at any time in many locations

ATM machines can be dangerous
      may be robbed getting money from machine

Banks store a lot of private information about consumers

If there is a mistake, it is difficult to get it corrected

To evaluate effects is to determine the value or benefit of the effects. In general, we ask whether the effects are positive or negative, if they are good or bad.

ACTIVITY 8-2   Look at the list you made in Activity 8-1. Determine if most of the effects are positive or negative. Then, fill in the chart on the next page. Here is an example:

TOPIC: COMPUTERS IN THE BANKING INDUSTRY

POSITIVE EFFECTS	NEGATIVE EFFECTS
transactions are fast, easy, convenient—both at banks and at ATM machines	ATM machines may be dangerous
	banks have personal information
	hard to correct mistakes

YOUR TOPIC:

POSITIVE EFFECTS	NEGATIVE EFFECTS

Expanding a Paragraph into an Essay

A paragraph is a small unit of writing that focuses on one idea. Sometimes a topic is too complex or broad for a single paragraph, so the writer expands the discussion of the topic into several paragraphs, into an essay. An **essay** is an expanded discussion of a single topic. It contains the same parts as a paragraph:

introduction (topic sentence)
support
conclusion

In an essay, each of these parts is expanded into one or more paragraphs.

ACTIVITY 8-3   Read the following paragraph. Write the topic, controlling idea, and points of support below.

The Advantages of a Microwave Oven

Microwave ovens have made our busy lives easier. First, microwave ovens are fast. They cook food much faster than regular ovens.

Second, they are convenient. Microwaves are really easy to use. Finally, they are safe. You don't have to worry about fires. With these advantages, the microwave has become a standard piece of equipment in many places.

Topic: _____

Controlling Idea: _____

Support: _____

_____

_____

The three points given in the paragraph in Activity 8-3 support the controlling idea, but the support is limited. The writer needs to give more details and examples to support the points.

ACTIVITY 8-4   Think of more details and examples the writer could add to support each point. Write two or three sentences for each point.

1. First, microwave ovens are fast.

   They cook food much faster than regular ovens.

   _____

   _____

   _____

2. Second, they are convenient.

   Microwaves are really easy to use.

   _____

   _____

   _____

3. Finally, they are safe.

   You don't have to worry about fires.

   _____

   _____

   _____

The writer could use the details and examples you have suggested in this activity to expand the paragraph into an essay. In this expansion, each point of support would become a separate paragraph in the body, or main part, of the essay.

ACTIVITY 8-5 Read the following essay that was expanded from the paragraph on pages 178–179. Answer the questions that follow.

The Advantages of a Microwave Oven

Engineers and inventors continually develop new products that affect our everyday lives. One product that was developed and has become popular in the last twenty years is the microwave oven. Microwave ovens now appear in new homes, old homes, businesses, restaurants, even on boats and in campers. Indeed, they are everywhere. Most people would agree that this invention, with its many advantages, has had a positive effect on our lives. It has made our busy lives easier.

The most important advantage of the microwave is speed. It cooks food much faster than a conventional oven. A box of frozen broccoli takes six minutes to cook on a stove. In the microwave, it only takes two minutes. That is one-third the time of the regular method. This advantage of the microwave oven—speed—is important in our daily lives. Since most adults work, they do not have much time to spend preparing dinner for their families. Now, when the children come home from school or the adults come home from their jobs, an entire dinner can be fixed in a very short time with the help of the microwave.

The second advantage of the microwave is convenience. The microwave is really easy to use. You put a frozen pizza on a plate, pop it in the microwave, push a couple of buttons and presto! you have a hot meal. It is so easy to use that children and teenagers can use it with no trouble. If children want an after-school snack, they can fix it themselves. There is no mess and no fuss. It is not only easy to use at home, but also in offices. Many offices have an employee lounge where employees can eat lunch. A common feature of the lounge is a microwave oven. Employees can bring soup, leftovers, or entire meals and heat them up in the microwave in a couple of minutes. This is a quick, convenient way to have a hot **nourishing**° lunch.

healthy

Another advantage of the microwave is safety. Because the microwave oven heats food with microwaves instead of with fire, you don't have to worry about starting a fire or getting burned when you are cooking. This is especially important with children. Children love to help their parents cook and may even try to cook when the parents are gone. If children use the microwave, their parents don't have to worry about fires.

These advantages have quickly made the microwave oven a standard piece of equipment in homes, apartments, offices, restaurants, dormitory rooms, campers, boats—almost any place that people spend time. The microwave oven is one invention that has quickly become a part of our lives.

1. What are the three advantages of a microwave oven? Underline the sentences that state these three main advantages.
2. What details does the writer use to support these advantages? Are any of them the same as you suggested in Activity 8-4?

The Parts of an Essay

An essay has the same parts as a paragraph: an introduction, support, and conclusion. Notice that the structure of an essay is similar to the structure of a paragraph. Compare the parts in each:

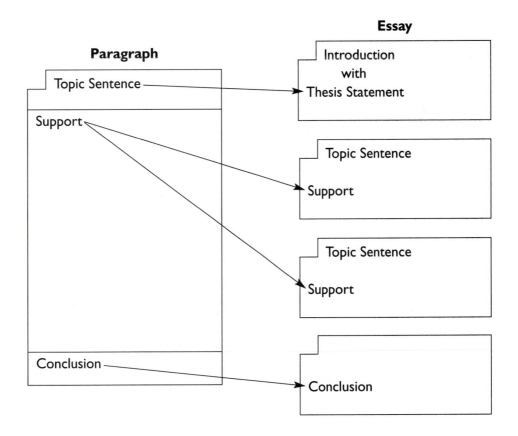

The Thesis Statement

The **thesis statement** is the main-idea sentence for the entire essay. It gives the attitude, opinion, or idea that the writer is going to develop in the essay. Like a topic sentence, the thesis statement tells the topic and controlling idea. Unlike a topic sentence, it controls the whole essay, not just one paragraph.

An essay has an overall thesis statement to focus its main idea. At the same time, the supporting paragraphs of the essay have topic sentences. These topic sentences relate to and develop some aspect of the controlling idea of the essay.

The following guidelines will help you recognize and write a thesis statement.

1. A thesis statement must be a complete sentence.
   The benefits of the computer. (Not a thesis statement)
   The computer can help students do research. (Thesis statement)

2. A thesis statement gives an opinion, attitude, or idea; it should not just announce the topic of the essay.
   I am going to discuss the effects of VCRs. (Not a thesis statement)
   VCRs have increased the choices for viewers. (Thesis statement)

3. A thesis statement is more interesting when it expresses an opinion, not a fact, because facts cannot be argued.
   Most aluminum cans have flip tops. (Not a thesis statement)
   Flip tops make aluminum cans hard to open. (Thesis statement)

4. A thesis statement is not a question (but will often be the answer to a question).
   What are the advantages of credit cards? (Not a thesis statement)
   Credit cards are convenient. (Thesis statement)

ACTIVITY 8-6   Using the guidelines above, decide if the following phrases and sentences are thesis statements. Rewrite those that are incorrect, making them thesis statements.

1. The disadvantages of power windows in cars. _____

   _____

2. What are the effects of kidney transplants? _____

   _____

3. I would like to tell you about my experience with video games. _____

   _____

4. Without basic computer skills, it is difficult to use the library. _____

   _____

5. Frozen foods are not nearly as tasty as fresh foods. _____

   _____

6. How are computers used in the hotel industry? _____

_____

7. Fast food restaurants are designed to serve customers quickly. _____

_____

8. Some athletes use drugs to build up their bodies. _____

_____

ACTIVITY 8-7   Brainstorm ideas for essays on the general topics below. Then write a thesis statement for each topic. Your thesis statement should be a complete sentence and should tell both the topic and the controlling idea. The first one is done as an example.

1. exercising

Thesis statement: Regular exercise has great benefits for elderly people.

2. television advertising _____

_____

3. owning a car_____

_____

4. the school library_____

_____

5. high-speed trains_____

_____

6. cellular telephones_____

_____

The Introduction

An essay has an introduction of one or more paragraphs. The number of paragraphs in the introduction depends upon the length and complexity of the essay. Short essays (up to ten typed pages) usually have just one introductory paragraph.

The following characteristics will help you evaluate and write an introduction.

1. The introduction should be inviting. It should be interesting enough to make the reader want to continue reading. The writer's job is to "hook" the reader—to get the reader so interested in the topic and the writer's idea about the topic that the reader will want to read the entire essay.

2. The introduction gives the following:
the topic—what the essay is about
the thesis statement—the writer's attitude or idea about the topic

3. The thesis statement can appear any place in the introduction. Often, however, the thesis statement is the last sentence of the introduction.

Traditionally, the introductory paragraph of an essay is represented as an inverted triangle. The paragraph begins by introducing the general idea of the topic and narrows to the specific idea of the thesis statement. This is why the thesis statement is often the last sentence of the introduction. Look at this diagram:

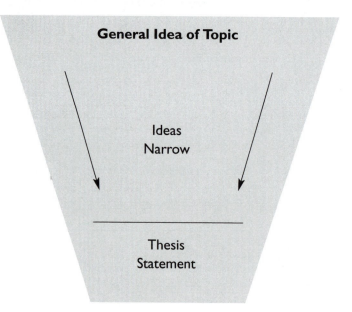

Look at the introductory paragraph of the essay about microwave ovens. Find the thesis statement.

Engineers and inventors continually develop new products that affect our everyday lives. One product that was developed and has become popular in the last twenty years is the microwave oven. Microwave ovens now appear in new homes, old homes, businesses, restaurants, even on boats and in campers. Indeed, they are everywhere. Most people would agree that this invention, with its many advantages, has had a positive effect on our lives. It has made our busy lives easier.

The last sentence of the paragraph presents the thesis, or main idea, the writer is going to develop. This statement tells us what to expect in the essay. We expect the essay to answer this question, "How has the microwave made our busy lives easier?"

Notice that the writer has used the inverted triangle approach in this introduction. The introduction begins with the general idea that new products affect our lives. It narrows down to the more specific idea that one product, the microwave oven, has a particular effect on our lives, making our lives easier.

One way to write this kind of introduction is to use in the thesis sentence a key word or idea that was used in the first sentence of the paragraph. In the paragraph above, the writer uses the phrase *affect our everyday lives* in the first sentence. This idea is repeated in the thesis sentence: *made our busy lives easier.*

ACTIVITY 8-8   Read the following introductory paragraphs. For each one, answer these questions:

1. Is the paragraph inviting?
2. What is the topic it introduces?
3. What is the thesis statement?
4. Is the paragraph an inverted triangle?

1.   As we know, language is the most important means of communication. Without it, we human beings seem like other animals, like monkeys or elephants. Most countries around the world have their own language; however, English is a world language because it is spoken by millions of people in the Western Hemisphere, Asia, and Africa. Especially to foreign students and immigrants or refugees who settle in the U.S.A., English has become essential to communicate with native people.

—Bachvan Doan

2.   Computers are a wonderful invention. They have spread out from businesses to most families and have become very popular. In most jobs, computers have been used as efficient and reliable workers. They can remember enormous amounts of information and retrieve data in a very short time. For this reason, computers can save people a lot of time.

—Truong Dinh

3.   Today, computers are a part of our daily lives in almost every area. In education, especially in high school and college, students nowadays are equipped with computers to make their lives easier and their education more progressive. Using a word processor in writing, accessing the school or library via a computer network or modem, getting an e-mail—these are only a few of the ways that computers are useful to students.

—Luan Ngo

The Support

The supporting paragraphs of the essay all relate to the thesis statement. Each paragraph discusses one aspect of the main idea. This aspect is generally stated in a topic sentence. The paragraph then supports the main idea by giving facts, details, examples, or an explanation. Think again about the essay on the advantages of the microwave. Each of its body paragraphs discussed one aspect of the thesis statement.

ACTIVITY 8-9   Choose one of the thesis statements you developed in Activity 8-7. Brainstorm again and write out at least three topic sentences you could use to support the thesis statement. List possible facts, details, and examples you could use to support the topic sentences.

The Conclusion

An essay usually has a concluding paragraph. This paragraph brings the essay to a close in a logical way.

The following characteristics will help you evaluate and write a conclusion. A conclusion can:

1. briefly restate the main points of the essay
2. restate the thesis of the essay
3. make a prediction
4. return to the general idea the essay started with

For example, the essay about the microwave concludes by restating the thesis of the essay.

ACTIVITY 8-10   Read the following essay written by a student and answer the questions that follow.

Why Life Without a Car in the U.S. Is Difficult

On a street in New Orleans, a middle-aged man sitting on a bench in a bus shelter is waiting for a bus. He occasionally glances at his watch. He sits waiting impatiently for the bus to come. Sometimes he stands up and looks to the corner of the street, hoping to see the bus. Finally, he sees a bus coming. Unfortunately, it is full of people, so he has to wait for the next one. As you can see, this man waits impatiently for a bus. If he had a car, he probably would not be so impatient. Indeed, not having a car in the U.S. is difficult. There may be several effects, but two stand out.

First of all, you have no means of transportation when you need to go somewhere. In daily life, you have to go many places—to work, to school, to the bank, or to the store. Not all of these places are near your home. So you can hardly get to these places if you do not have a car. Although you can take the bus, bus lines are not always next to your home. In brief, having your own car to transport you is much more convenient than taking a bus. For example, one of my friends, Hung, who lives on the West Bank, needed to go to the drug store one day. His car was broken, so he was without transportation at that time. He also could not go by bus because the nearest bus line was about two miles away from his home. Finally, he decided not to go to the store.

You not only have no means of transportation, but you also waste your time and money if you go by bus. As I said, you can take a bus even though it is not very convenient. However, it will cost you a lot of time and money. I, for instance, used to go to school by bus because I did not have a car. Once, when I had already got on a bus to go to school, I remembered leaving my English book at home. So I got off the bus, waited at a bus-stop for about twenty minutes, and got on another bus to go back to my home. I found my book at home, and, again after about fifteen minutes of waiting, I boarded another bus to go to school. In short, I wasted thirty-five minutes and two dollars in total just because I forgot my book at home. If I had had a car, I certainly would not have wasted such time and money.

In conclusion, having a car in the U.S. is very necessary for you. If you have a car, you can go promptly to any place you need to go. Not only is it convenient for you, but it is helpful for your family as well. You and your family can go together anywhere without wasting a lot of money and time.

—Hoang Vo

1. Is the introductory paragraph inviting? Does it introduce the topic?
2. Underline the thesis statement. Is it clear?
3. Underline the topic sentences. Do they support the thesis sentence?
4. What kind of support does the writer use?
5. Does the support in the paragraphs support the topic sentences?
6. Does the conclusion end the discussion logically?

ACTIVITY 8-11   Using the topic you worked on in Activity 8-9, write the essay.

Writing

Writing Assignment 1: Essay Evaluating Effects

Now you are going to write an essay evaluating effects. You are going to determine the particular effects of a recent invention or innovation and evaluate them. In other words, you are going to determine the advantages or disadvantages of something. (You can choose another topic if your teacher agrees.)

1. PREPARE TO WRITE.

   A. First, think of a topic. Following are some examples. You might think of others.

      The Effects of an Invention or Innovation in Modern Life

      Video games

      Credit cards

      Cellular telephones

      Palm Pilots

      Robots in industry

      Lasers

      Artificial organs

      Electronic banking

      VCRs

      Velcro

      Ultrasound

      Digital cameras

   B. After you have decided on your topic, get ideas by using one of the methods listed in Appendix B. You may want to brainstorm or make a list. Ask yourself these questions:

      What are the particular effects of _____?
      How do I evaluate these effects? Or,
      What are the advantages and disadvantages of _____?

   C. Decide on a controlling idea and write a thesis statement.

   D. Think about support for your controlling idea. List possible points and supporting details and examples.

   E. Organize your points in a logical way.

   F. Think about an interesting way to introduce your topic. Remember your audience.

2. WRITE THE ESSAY.

3. REVISE THE ESSAY.

    A. Ask a partner to evaluate your essay using the Paragraph Guidelines, or do it yourself using the Revising Checklist.

    B. Revise your essay.

Paragraph Guidelines
1. Write out the thesis statement and list the topic sentences.
2. Do the topic sentences support the thesis statement?
3. Does the support in the paragraphs support the topic sentences?
4. Are there enough examples and details to support the major points? If not, where would you like more support?
5. What part of the essay did you especially like?
6. What part would you like to know more about?
7. Has the writer made the essay interesting to the reader?

Revising Guidelines
1. Is your introduction inviting? Does it introduce the topic?
2. Do you have a clear thesis? Does it give the main idea of the entire essay?
3. Do your topic sentences support the thesis statement?
4. Does the support you give in each paragraph support the topic sentence?
5. Do you give enough examples and details to support the major points?
6. Do you conclude the essay logically?
7. Is your essay interesting?

Using Language Effectively

Cohesion: Connecting Words to Connect Paragraphs

Like a paragraph, an essay must be cohesive. Each paragraph must flow smoothly, and there must be smooth connections between the body paragraphs. One way to achieve this is to use key words and sentence connectors to connect the body paragraphs.

Look again at the essay on pages 180–181. What words and phrases connect the paragraphs of the essay?

The first body paragraph is introduced with the phrase _____

_____

The second body paragraph is introduced with the phrase _____

_____

The third body paragraph is introduced with the phrase_____

_____

The following connecting words will give cohesion to your essay.

WORDS TO INDICATE EVALUATION

KEY WORDS

the first advantage of

　　　　benefit of

　　　　reason that

one disadvantage of

another problem with

the last/final reason that

the most important/significant benefit of

Examples

One disadvantage of computers is the time it takes to learn how to use them.

Another disadvantage of computers is their expense.

The most significant disadvantage of computers is their dependence on electricity to function.

WORDS TO INDICATE SEQUENCE OF EXAMPLES OR POINTS

SENTENCE CONNECTORS

first

second

also

finally

most important

Examples

First, computers take time to learn how to use.

Also, computers are expensive.

Most important, computers are dependent on electricity to function.

ACTIVITY 8-12   Using the connecting words above, write three topic sentences on the advantages or disadvantages of credit cards.

Grammar Review

The following grammar points will help you write essays evaluating effects. If you want to review them, turn to the pages listed below.

Adverbial Clauses of Result   Page 263
Reduced Adverbial Clauses   Page 265

Using the Internet

INTERNET ACTIVITY   Many Web sites have information on the effects of technology. For example, you can find out the effects of technology on music, on middle school students, and on communities. Use a search engine such as Google, Yahoo!, or Excite to find a Web site that gives information about the effects of technology on something or someone, and do the following.

1. Choose a topic and read about it.
2. On a separate sheet of paper, write some notes about the effects of technology on the topic you have chosen.
3. If the Web site evaluates the effects, write down the evaluation.
4. Using your notes, explain your information to a partner or your classmates and teacher. While speaking, use connecting words to indicate evaluation.
5. Compare the effects of technology you have found with those of your partner's or classmates'. Can you find similarities and differences? What are they? Are the evaluations of the effects mostly positive or mostly negative?
6. Your teacher may ask you to write a paragraph explaining the information you found on evaluating the effects of technology on something or someone.

Preparing to Write

Outlining an Essay

An **outline** is the basic structure or skeleton of an essay. It includes all of the main ideas and details of the essay. It shows how the parts of the essay relate to each other.

An outline is useful as a way to organize an essay. A writer can use an outline as a basic plan to write an essay. Or a writer can outline an essay after it is written to make sure that the essay is unified and coherent.

The basic method for outlining an essay is as follows:

Thesis statement:

Write out the thesis statement in a complete sentence.

    I. Write out the first supporting topic sentence.

        A. Identify the support. This can be an idea, detail, or example that the paragraph will discuss.

            1. Give a detail about A.

            2. Give an additional detail about A.

        B. If you have another detail or example to discuss in this paragraph, do it here.

    II. Write out the next topic sentence.

        A. Support.

        B. Support.

        C. Details as appropriate.

    III. Write out the next topic sentence.

        A. Support.

        B. Support.

        C. Support.

Conclusion:

Study the following outline of the microwave essay:

Thesis statement: It has made our busy lives easier.

    I. The most important advantage of the microwave is speed.

        A. It cooks faster than a conventional oven.

            1. example—frozen broccoli

        B. Effect on our daily lives

            1. adults

            2. children

    II. The second advantage of the microwave is convenience.

        A. The microwave is really easy to use.

            1. at home

                a. example—frozen pizza

                b. easy for children—after-school snack

            2. at the office

                a. employees can fix a quick, nutritious lunch

    III. Another advantage of the microwave is safety.

        A. Uses microwaves, not fire

        B. Effect—don't have to worry

            1. starting a fire

            2. getting burned

        C. Especially important for children

Conclusion: These advantages have made the microwave a part of our busy lives.

ACTIVITY 8-13   Using the form given above, outline the following essay.

The Advantages of Advertising

Living in a communist country, I had never known about advertising before I came to the United States. To me, it was hard to understand, since in Vietnam there were no advertisements on TV, on the radio, or in the newspapers. In capitalist nations, however, no one can avoid being influenced by advertising; it is everywhere. We find it not only in the media but also on buses, buildings, even on the clothes we wear. Like all things, advertising has two aspects: negative and positive. However, the positive aspects outweigh the negative. To me, there are many advantages of advertising, but I will mention only two: to stimulate business growth and to create jobs.

First, advertising is one of the principal factors in stimulating business growth. In capitalist countries, there are many factories and businesses making the same product. They must compete with each other to get the attention of the consumer and sell their product. To achieve this goal, they must invest money to advertise their product. If their advertising is successful and their sales go up, their business grows. They make huge profits which they can then invest. This investment stimulates the economy even more. This is how the capitalist system works. A good example of a company with a successful advertising campaign is Burger King. Burger King used to be a small company with not many customers, but several years ago it started putting clever ads on TV to try to get some of the fast food business from McDonald's. These ads made Burger King's hamburgers look as good or better than McDonald's. Today, you can see many more Burger Kings around the country with lots of customers.

One of the results of a stimulated economy is creation of jobs. If a company grows and must produce more, it needs more employees. It must employ workers at every level, from janitors to vice-presidents. This creates jobs for many people. As Burger King has grown, for example, it has hired many new people to fill both management and waiter jobs in its restaurants. An example of a local company that has grown and created jobs is the New Orleans Shirt Company. It is becoming famous for its elegant shirts, which are distributed all over the South. Although it only started five years ago, it has started to receive orders from Mervyn's, Maison Blanche, Dillard's, and even Polo. Therefore, it is hiring more people.

In summary, advertising is an essential incentive to develop and advance the capitalist economy. It is necessary to stimulate business growth and create jobs. Through advertising, companies grow and consumers are provided with information about products. Without advertising, the economy would stagnate and maybe even collapse. Thus, to me, advertising has many positive aspects.

—*Bachvan Doan*

Writing

Writing Assignment 2: Essay Evaluating Effects

Now you are going to write an essay evaluating effects. You can choose one of the topics listed below or a topic of your own choice.

1. PREPARE TO WRITE.

   A. First, think about a topic. Following are some possible topics. You might think of others.

      The Effects of an Action or Event in Your Life

      Moving away from your family

      Leaving your home country

      Learning a new language

      Changing jobs or taking a new job

      Making an important decision

      The Effects of People and Their Behavior

      Dropping out of school

      Divorce on a family

      Dependence on drugs

   B. After you have decided on your topic, get ideas by using one of the methods listed in Appendix B. You may want to brainstorm or make a list. Ask yourself these questions:

      What are the particular effects of _____?

      How do I evaluate these effects? Or,

      What are the advantages and disadvantages of _____?

   C. Decide on a controlling idea and write a thesis statement.

   D. Think about support for your controlling idea. List possible points and supporting details and examples.

   E. Organize your points in a logical way.

   F. Think about an interesting way to introduce your topic. Remember your audience.

G. Write an outline of your essay.

2. WRITE THE ESSAY.

3. REVISE THE ESSAY.

A. Use the Revising Checklist to evaluate your paper, or ask a partner to do it.

B. Revise your paper.

Revising Checklist

1. Is your introduction inviting? Does it introduce the topic?
2. Do you have a clear thesis? Does it give the main idea of the entire essay?
3. Do your topic sentences support the thesis?
4. Does the support you give in each paragraph support the topic sentence?
5. Do you give enough examples and details to support the major points?
6. Do you have smooth transitions within and between paragraphs?
7. Do you conclude the essay logically?
8. Is your essay interesting?

More Reading and Writing

Discuss these questions with your classmates or teacher.

1. Do parents worry about the safety of their small children? In what ways?
2. How could technology help parents keep their children safe?

Reading

Kid Finder

by Suzanne Kantra Kirschner

This article first appeared in *Popular Science* in 2001. It was written by Suzanne Kantra Kirschner.

It's 10:00 P.M. Do you know where your children are? Soon parents could know to within three meters, but only if their children are carrying Siemens' Leonie, a combination cell phone and GPS (Global Positioning System) receiver that can be integrated into a teddy bear, knapsack, or water bottle.

The Leonie is designed to help children ages four to twelve and their parents keep in touch. If a child misses the bus after school, for example, he or she can call a parent by pressing a green button. Doing so **initiates**° a call to the Child Call Center, which communicates with the child via a built-in speaker and then contacts the parent.

begins; causes to happen

In an emergency, the child presses the red button. A call is again initiated to the call center. In addition to communicating with the child, the center can determine an exact location from data passed along by Leonie's built-in GPS receiver, so police and emergency services can be **dispatched**° directly. The Leonie also enables the center to listen in if a dangerous situation, such as a kidnaping, is suspected. The operator can continually access data from the built-in GPS receiver to track a child as he or she moves.

sent out

Currently fifty families in Munich, Germany, are testing the device. Siemens hopes to begin selling the device in Europe by the end of the year and shortly thereafter in the United States.

Meanwhile, a company called Wherify Wireless plans to offer a similar service in the near future. The company's watch-style Personal Location System, which users wear, has a built-in GPS receiver and can send out 911 distress calls and receive text messages.

Comprehension. Answer the following questions.

1. What is the Leonie?
2. How does it work?
3. What are the advantages of the Leonie in a normal situation?
4. What are the advantages of the Leonie in an emergency?
5. How does the Leonie differ from the product offered by Wherify Wireless?
6. What is the major effect the writer discusses in the reading?
7. What kind of support does the writer use? Does she use facts, details, examples? Find the support and tell what kind it is.
8. Evaluate the support. Which support do you think is most effective? Why?

Discussion. Discuss these questions with your classmates or teacher.

1. Can you think of any disadvantages of the Leonie? What are they?
2. If you had children, would you use the Leonie? Why or why not?

Discussion. Discuss the following questions with your classmates or teacher.

1. What do archeologists do?
2. What tools do they use to do their work?
3. What technological innovation might make their work easier?

Reading

object from the past

High-Tech Relic° Hunting
by Michael Carroll

This article first appeared in *Popular Science* in 2001. It was written by Michael Carroll.

(verb) make a picture of

The tedious, backbreaking work of sifting through soil at archaeological sites may soon be a thing of the past. Researchers at the University of Illinois at Urbana-Champaign are using sound waves to **image**° buried objects before any digging begins.

"It used to be that a researcher would take a shovelful of dirt and sift it through a grate," explains William O'Brien, a professor of engineering. "That is a very time-consuming process."

pattern of sounds

O'Brien and his colleagues, with the backing of the Army Corps of Engineers, are developing an **acoustic array**° that sends pulses of sound into the ground and then picks up the sound waves reflected by buried objects. A computer converts the reflections into an image. The array, adapted from a torpedo head, is one of a new generation of instruments designed to do **noninvasive**° archaeology.

not requiring that objects be cut or broken into

These new instruments can be used to create detailed site maps revealing the depth and location of buried objects, foundations, and other structures. Such maps save time and money by limiting **excavation**° to areas of interest.

digging to find buried objects

Ground-penetrating° radar is well suited for finding metallic objects, but is limited in **resolution**° and does not work well in wet soil. The new acoustic system is better at imaging small objects and can detect nonmetallic **artifacts**° such as pottery shards and stone tools.

passing through the ground

the clarity of a picture

very old objects once used by humans

The acoustic system won't replace radar and shovels; it merely gives archaeologists another tool to use, says O'Brien. "In medicine, doctors use multiple techniques for a diagnosis. The principle is the same here."

Comprehension. Answer the following questions.

1. What kind of waves are used in the system described here?
2. What is the purpose of the new system?
3. How does the system work?
4. What are the advantages of the new system?
5. How is this system better than ground-penetrating radar?
6. What are the major effects of the new system?

Discussion. Discuss these questions with your classmates or teacher.

1. Can you think of any disadvantages of the acoustic system? What are they?
2. Can you think of any advantages of the system that are not mentioned in the article? What are they?
3. This system is adapted from a torpedo head, an instrument of war. Can you think of any other technologies that were designed for war but later were adapted for peacetime use? What are they?

Topics for Discussion and Writing

Your teacher may ask you to discuss or write about one of the following topics:

1. The effects of being unemployed on a person or family
2. The effects of getting older or becoming a certain age
3. The effects of an attitude (racial prejudice, fear of AIDS, love, caring, pity) on a person or group of people
4. The effects of living in a consumer society
5. The effects of a certain type of parent on children

Appendices

Appendix A: Map of the World

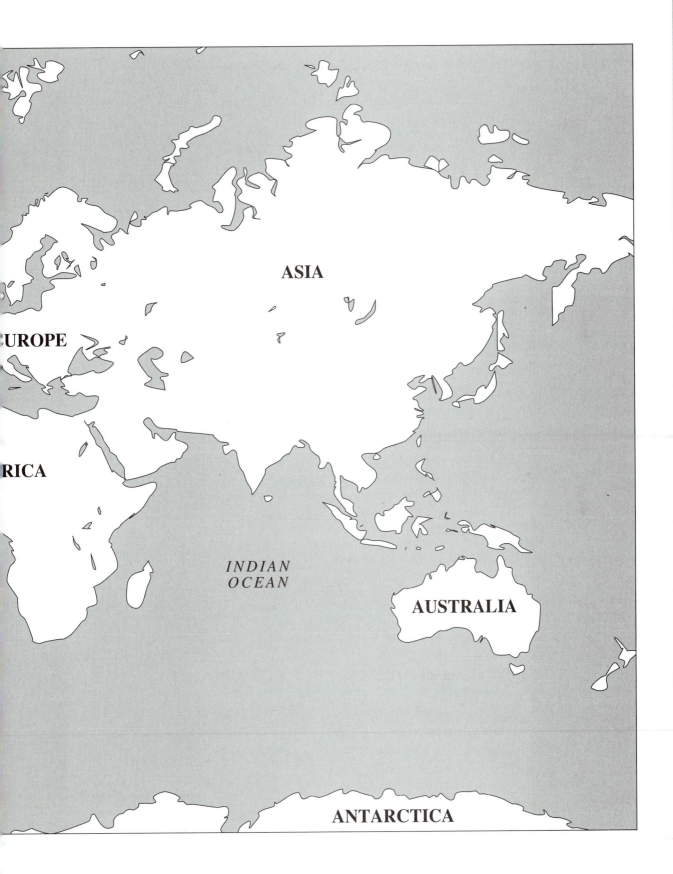

Appendix B: Strategies for Getting Ideas

Following are some ways to help you get ideas for writing.

Brainstorming

Follow these steps to brainstorm about your topic:

1. Write your topic on a piece of paper. The topic can be a word, a phrase, or a question.
2. Write down *any* ideas that come to mind. Write quickly without evaluating your ideas.

Here is an example of brainstorming:

Coming to this Country
> study computer science
> get a job
> leave home
> miss my family
> strange food
> must speak English
> make new friends

3. After you have listed as many ideas as you can, read over the list and circle the ideas you might want to use in your writing.

Making a List

Follow these steps to make a list:

1. Write your topic on a piece of paper.
2. Think about your topic and write down any good ideas that come to mind.

Here is an example of a list:

A Time I Learned a Lesson
> 12 years old
> teacher assigned descriptive essay
> didn't want to do it
> played soccer with my friends
> my team won the soccer game

six of us copied essay from friend
teacher kept our essays
called us to blackboard
hit us on palms five times with ruler
called our parents
no soccer for one month
never copied again

3. After you have made a list, read over the list and choose the ideas you want to include in your writing.

Drawing a Sketch

Drawing a sketch is a good way to get ideas and details to describe a person or place. Follow these steps to draw a sketch:

1. Write your topic on a piece of paper.
2. Draw a brief sketch or diagram of the person or place you are describing. Don't worry if you are not an artist; draw the person or place to help you remember.

Here is an example of a sketch:

My Grandmother's Back Yard

3. After you have drawn your sketch, use it to help you write about the place.

Freewriting

Freewriting is a way to loosen your mind and let your ideas flow. Follow these steps to freewrite:

1. Choose a topic you want to write about.
2. Write quickly about the topic for five or ten minutes. Don't worry about spelling or grammar. If you can't think of a word in English, write it in your language. The important thing is to keep writing.
3. If you can't think of anything to write, write the same thing over again.

Here is an example of freewriting:

My Grandmother's Back Yard

I remember this place very well. I used to sit on the steps and look at it. It was always green in the summer with bushes on all sides—there was a big lilac bush in the back on the left with a huge oak tree in the back on the right. I used to crawl under the lilac bush and hide—it was dark and smelled like earth. I pretended it was my house, I felt protected under there. I tried to climb the oak tree but I couldn't reach the first limb. In the fall, when the leaves fell, we raked the leaves and rolled around in the piles—they smelled so good.

4. When you have finished writing, read over your freewriting. Circle the ideas you might want to use in your writing.

Making a Venn Diagram

Making a Venn diagram will help you compare and contrast. Follow these steps to make a Venn diagram:

1. Draw two big overlapping circles.
2. In the center, where the circles overlap, list the ways in which the two things you are comparing are alike.
3. In the two outer circles, list the ways that they are different.

Here is an example of a Venn diagram:

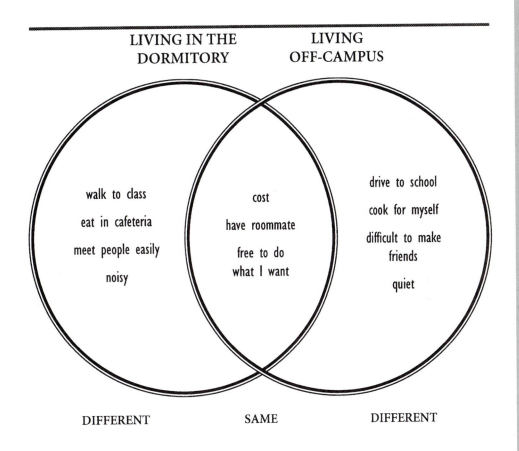

LIVING IN THE DORMITORY		LIVING OFF-CAMPUS
walk to class	cost	drive to school
eat in cafeteria	have roommate	cook for myself
meet people easily	free to do what I want	difficult to make friends
noisy		quiet
DIFFERENT	SAME	DIFFERENT

4. When you have finished making the diagram, decide which points of comparison/contrast you want to write about.

Clustering

Clustering is a way to help you see your ideas on paper. It helps you to see connections between main ideas and supporting details. Follow these steps to cluster:

1. Write your topic in the middle of a piece of paper. Circle it.
2. Think about your topic. Write down each idea you have about the topic in a smaller circle. Draw a line from the smaller circles to the big circle in the center.
3. Now think about the ideas in the smaller circles. Write down any ideas you have about them, circle them, and connect them to the smaller circles.

Here is an example of clustering:

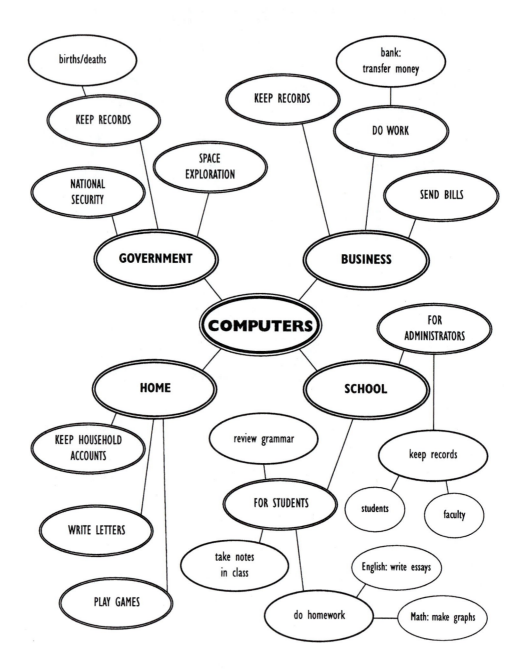

4. When you have finished clustering, read over your ideas. Decide which ones you want to use in your writing.

Appendix C-1: Grammar Review, Chapter 1

Clauses

In English, the basic unit of writing is the sentence. Sentences are made up of clauses. A **clause** is a group of words with at least a subject and a verb. Sometimes a clause also has a complement, a group of words following the verb that completes the idea of the sentence.

CLAUSES

SUBJECT	VERB	COMPLEMENT	
Parents	should encourage	their children.	(clause)
I	received	a reward.	(clause)
I	was	happy.	(clause)
I	passed.		(clause)
my lazy brother	(not a clause—no verb)		
refused to go to class	(not a clause—no subject)		
last week.	(not a clause— no subject or verb)		

There are two kinds of clauses: independent clauses and dependent clauses.

Independent Clauses

An **independent clause** has a subject and verb *and* can stand by itself. It can be a sentence; it is complete.

Businesses advertise many products.
They advertise cars, food, clothes, books, and music.

ACTIVITY C-1-1   The clauses below are all independent clauses. For each one, do the following:

1. Circle the subject.
2. Underline the verb.
3. Put two lines under the complement.

The first one is done as an example.

1. (Restaurant advertising) has <u>several advantages</u>.
2. It gives customers information about the restaurant.

3. The information can include the type of food.

4. It can give the location and hours of the restaurant.

5. It might tell about a famous chef.

6. Advertising also makes the restaurant familiar to people.

7. Advertising repeats the name of the restaurant many times.

8. The name becomes familiar to everyone.

9. People think the restaurant is a good one.

Coordinators

Often, we combine two independent clauses to make one sentence. There are three ways to do this. One way is to combine the clauses with a small word called a *coordinator*. The coordinator is placed at the beginning of the second clause. A comma is usually placed after the first clause.

The coordinator shows the relationship between the two clauses. The writer chooses the one that will best serve his or her purpose.

COORDINATORS

WRITER'S PURPOSE	COORDINATORS
To add an idea	and
To show contrast	but, yet
To present a choice	or, nor
To indicate result	so
To indicate reason	for*

INDEPENDENT CLAUSE	COORDINATOR	INDEPENDENT CLAUSE
I hid behind my mother,	**and**	I did not look at the teacher.

(**, and** indicates additional information is coming)

I wanted to talk to her,	**but**	I was afraid.

(**, but** indicates contrasting information is coming)

I could tell the teacher,	**or**	I could suffer in silence.

(**, or** indicates a choice is coming)

The school was near my house,	**so**	it only took five minutes to walk there.

(**, so** indicates a result of the first clause is coming)

* The word *for* is not commonly used as a coordinator to indicate reason, it is more common to use *because*.

ACTIVITY C-1-2 Each of the sentences below has two independent clauses. Do the following.

1. For each clause, circle the subject, underline the verb, and put two lines under the complement.
2. In each sentence, circle the coordinator and the comma twice.
3. Then tell the relationship between the two clauses: addition, contrast, choice, result.

The first one is done as an example.

1. (I) have <u>many friends</u>, (but) (my best friend) is <u>Paul</u>. *contrast*
2. Paul and I met in high school, and we have been friends ever since.
3. In high school, we studied the same subjects, and we often studied together.
4. Paul was particularly good at English, so he often helped me with that subject.
5. I liked math a lot, and I often helped Paul with that.
6. After school, we often played soccer with the other boys, or we went to a popular restaurant to have coffee.
7. Now, Paul is attending college in a different city, so we don't see each other very often.
8. However, we call each other almost every week, and we talk for a long time.
9. Paul has been a good friend to me, and I hope I have been a good friend to him.

The Semicolon

Another way to combine two independent clauses is to use a semicolon. The semicolon is used when the ideas in the two clauses are closely related. The combined clauses make one sentence.

THE SEMICOLON

INDEPENDENT CLAUSE	SEMICOLON	INDEPENDENT CLAUSE
My favorite activity is tennis	;	I play at least once a day.
Golf is a popular sport in my country	;	everyone plays.

Notice that the first word in the second clause is not capitalized.

ACTIVITY C-1-3 Each of the sentences below has two independent clauses, but they are not properly punctuated. Do the following:

1. For each clause, circle the subject, underline the verb, and put two lines under the complement.
2. Put a semicolon between the two independent clauses.

The first one is done as an example.

1. (My hobby) is <u>camping</u>; (I) <u>love</u> <u>to be outdoors</u>.
2. I go camping during my school holidays it helps me relax.
3. My favorite camping spot is in the mountains it has a wonderful view.
4. During the day I take a hike at night I build a fire and cook dinner.
5. After dinner I look at the stars and dream I feel so peaceful.

Transitional Words

Often, when using a semicolon to combine two clauses, a writer will also include a word called a **transitional word** (sometimes called a *conjunctive adverb*). This is a third way to connect clauses. The transitional word is placed at the beginning of the second clause and is followed by a comma.

Like coordinators, transitional words show the relationship of the ideas in the two clauses. The writer chooses the word that best indicates the relationship of ideas. Following are three common transitional words.

TRANSITIONAL WORDS

WRITER'S PURPOSE	TRANSITIONAL WORD
To add an idea	moreover
To indicate a result	therefore
To indicate an unexpected result	however

INDEPENDENT CLAUSE	TRANSITIONAL WORDS	INDEPENDENT CLAUSE
During my last holiday I had to study for exams;	**therefore,**	I couldn't go camping.

(; *therefore,* indicates a result of the first clause is coming)

I studied hard;	**however,**	I made time to see my friends.

(; *however,* indicates an unexpected result is coming)

We often went out dancing at night;	**moreover,**	we went to the beach on weekends.

(; *moreover,* indicates additional information is coming)

ACTIVITY C-1-4   Read the sentences below and do the following.

1. For each clause, circle the subject, underline the verb, and put two lines under the complement.

2. Then rewrite the sentence, connecting the two clauses with a semicolon and a transitional word. Put a comma after the transitional word. Use these transitional words: *therefore, however, moreover.*

3. Tell the relationship between the two clauses: result, unexpected result, addition.

The first one is done as an example.

1. In the United States, (many young people) <u>do not like</u> <u>to read the newspaper</u>.

(Reading the paper) is <u>very important to me.</u>

In the United States many young people do not like to read the newspaper;

however, reading the paper is very important to me.

__unexpected result__

2. It is the best way of getting information about world events.
   It has a lot of entertaining sections.

   _____

   _____

   _____

3. Knowing about world events is most important.
   I read the front page and the world news section first.

   _____

   _____

   _____

4. I also enjoy sports and comics.
   I read those sections next.

   _____

   _____

   _____

5. I like to do the crossword puzzle.
   Sometimes I don't have time for it.

   _____

   _____

   _____

6. I learn a lot from reading the paper.
   It is a relaxing way to spend my time.

   _____

   _____

   _____

Following is a list of common transitional words.

TRANSITIONAL WORDS

WRITER'S PURPOSE	TRANSITIONAL WORDS
To add an idea	moreover, in addition, also, furthermore, besides
To show time or sequence	first, second, next, then, finally
To indicate result	therefore, thus, consequently, as a result
To indicate unexpected result	however, nervertheless, still
To show contrast	however, on the other hand, in contrast, conversely
To show similarity	similarly, likewise
To emphasize or intensify	in fact, indeed, on the contrary
To give an example	for example, for instance
To explain or restate	that is, in other words
To generalize	in general, overall
To summarize	in conclusion, in summary

ACTIVITY C-1-5   Choose one of the following topics to write about:

the advantages of some type of advertising
your best friend
your favorite activity
an important city in your country

1. Write six pairs of sentences about the topic. Each sentence should have only one clause. The sentences in each pair should be related to each other.

2. Exchange papers with a partner and do the following:
   a. For each clause, circle the subject, underline the verb, and put two lines under the complement.
   b. Combine the clauses, using one of these: a coordinator, a semicolon alone, or a semicolon plus transitional word.

Example: (Seoul) <u>is</u> the capital of South Korea. (It) <u>has many government</u> <u>office buildings and embassies.</u>

Seoul is the capital of South Korea. It has many government office buildings and embassies.

Seoul is the capital of South Korea; therefore, it has many government office buildings and embassies.

You can also use transitional words between two sentences. In this case the first sentence is followed by a period, and the second sentence begins with the transitional word followed by a comma. The second sentence also begins with a capital letter.

Abidjan is one of the largest cities in west Africa. **Moreover,** it has many modern office buildings.

It has an excellent port. **Therefore,** it is a center for importing and exporting goods.

It is the economic center of Ivory Coast. **However,** it is not the capital of the country.

In this section, we have studied transitional words and used a lot of them for practice. However, when you write your paragraphs, you will not want to use too many transitional words. Often, you will only need one or two transitional words per paragraph or one between paragraphs. Your ideas should flow clearly from one sentence to the next. Use transitional words in order to help make your meaning clear to the reader.

Dependent Clauses

A **dependent** clause has a subject and a verb, but it *cannot* stand alone. A dependent clause is dependent because it has a particular type of word attached to it—called a **subordinator.** Thus, a dependent clause consists of a subordinator and an independent clause.

DEPENDENT CLAUSES

SUBORDINATOR + INDEPENDENT CLAUSE = DEPENDENT CLAUSE

When   I was charged with a crime

While   I was driving away

As soon as   I found out

The dependent clause is attached to an independent clause to make a sentence.

The dependent clause can occur before or after the independent clause. When the dependent clause comes at the beginning of the sentence, it is followed by a comma.

SENTENCES WITH DEPENDENT CLAUSES

DEPENDENT CLAUSE	INDEPENDENT CLAUSE

SUBORDINATOR + CLAUSE

When	**I was eight years old,**	I memorized a long poem.

INDEPENDENT CLAUSE	DEPENDENT CLAUSE

SUBORDINATOR + CLAUSE

I memorized a long poem	**when**	**I was eight years old.**

Following is a list of common subordinators.

SUBORDINATORS

WRITER'S PURPOSE	SUBORDINATOR
To indicate time	while, when, as, whenever, before, after, until, as soon as, the moment that, once
To show place	where
To indicate reason	because, since, now that, as long as
To show contrast	though, although, even though, while
To indicate result	so/such . . . that*

ACTIVITY C-1-6   The following sentences each have a dependent clause and an independent clause.

1. For each sentence, underline the dependent clause.
2. Circle the subordinator. If the dependent clause is at the beginning of the sentence, circle the comma following it.

   The first one is done as an example.

1. (When) I was in high school (,) my sister and I shared a car.
2. It was a big problem because we had different attitudes about it.
3. She liked to drive fast and was lazy about taking care of it while I wanted to be careful and take good care of it.
4. When I complained to my mother, she said we had to work it out between us.
5. Although I tried to talk to my sister about it, she just laughed and said I was too worried about it.

* You will study this subordinator in Appendix C-8.

6. I was really angry at her because she seemed so unreasonable.

7. One day, because my sister was driving fast, she had an accident.

8. Although she didn't get hurt in the accident, it really scared her and my whole family.

9. After she had the accident, she started to drive more carefully and I wasn't angry at her anymore.

ACTIVITY C-1-7   Read the sets of sentences below. Rewrite them, combining each set with a subordinator. You can change the order of the sentences if you want to.

1. Advertisements are good for manufacturing companies.
   They help companies tell how good their products are.

   _____

   _____

2. The Chrysler Corporation wants to show their new Jeep.
   They put an ad on TV that shows the Jeep driving on a rough road or climbing a mountain.

   _____

   _____

3. They show that.
   They want the consumer to know that their vehicle can drive on any kind of road.

   _____

   _____

4. Consumers see the ads.
   They go and buy the Jeep.

   _____

   _____

5. Advertisements help sell products.
   They are very expensive for the company.

   _____

   _____

6. Some television ads cost about $10,000 to produce.
   Others cost almost $100,000.

   _____

   _____

7. Companies must also pay to have the ads shown on TV.
   The cost is even higher.

   _____

   _____

8. We have many advertisements on TV.
   It must be worth it to the companies to advertise.

   _____

   _____

SUMMARY OF CONNECTING WORDS

WRITER'S PURPOSE	COORDINATORS	TRANSITIONAL WORDS	SUBORDINATORS
to add an idea	and	also moreover in addition besides furthermore	
to show contrast	but yet	however on the other hand in contrast conversely	though although even though while whereas
to show similarity		similarly likewise	
to present a choice	or nor		
to indicate result	so	therefore as a result thus consequently	so/such … that
to indicate unexpected result		however nevertheless still	

WRITER'S PURPOSE	COORDI-NATORS	TRANSITIONAL WORDS	SUBORDI-NATORS
to indicate reason	for		because since now that as long as
to give an example		for example for instance	
to emphasize or intensify		in fact indeed on the contrary	
to explain or restate		that is in other words	
to generalize		in general overall	
to summarize		in conclusion in summary	
to show time or sequence			first second next then finally meanwhile subsequently while when as whenever before after until as soon as the moment that once
to show place			where

To review **punctuation with transitional words,** see page 19 in Chapter 1 or study the sentences below.

Punctuation for coordinators with two independent clauses: a comma after the first clause.

I hid behind my mother, and I did not look at the teacher.

Punctuation for transitional words with two independent clauses: a semicolon after the first clause and a comma after the transitional word.

> During my last holiday I had to study for exams; therefore, I couldn't go camping.

Punctuation for transitional words with two sentences: a period after the first sentence and a comma after the transitional word.

> Abidjan is one of the largest cities in west Africa. Moreover, it has many modern office buildings.

Punctuation for subordinators with clauses: a comma after the dependent clause when it is before the independent clause. (There is no comma when the dependent clause is after the independent clause.)

> When I was eight years old, I memorized a long poem.
> It was a big problem because we had different attitudes about it.

Appendix C-2: Grammar Review, Chapter 2

Verb Tenses

Past Tense for Narrating

When a writer narrates, he or she usually is writing about something that happened in the past. To tell the story, the writer uses the **simple past tense** (**verb** + **-ed**).

SIMPLE PAST TENSE

Simple past tense is used to indicate:

general ideas and truths

Examples

I **was** eleven years old.

My classroom **had** a shelf made of wood.

habitual or completed action

Examples

My teacher **used** it to place miscellaneous things on.

The teacher **appeared** in the door.

mental perceptions or emotions

Examples

I **felt** afraid of the punishment.

I **thought** about my selfishness.

ACTIVITY C-2-1   Read the following paragraph from Hoang Vo's story, "My Fault." Underline the simple past tense verbs he uses to tell his story.

One day, when we were waiting for the teacher, my friend and I went to the shelf to look at the objects on it. We saw a toy car on top of the shelf and because it was too high to reach, my friend hung on the edge of the shelf and started to climb up. Suddenly his left hand collided with the flower vase. It fell on the floor with a little dry sound; the flower vase was broken into pieces.

Several other past tenses are used for special situations.

The **past perfect tense** (*had* + **past participle**) indicates a past event that happened before the past event the writer is discussing.

> Then she slowly turned her face to the class and asked in a trembling voice who **had broken** the vase.

The past perfect verb tense of *had broken* indicates that the vase was broken before the teacher spoke to the class.

The **past progressive tense** (*was* or *were* + **present participle**) is used to indicate an action in progress at a particular time in the past.

> One day, when we **were waiting** for the teacher, my friend and I went to the shelf to look at the objects on it.

The past progressive tense of *were waiting* indicates that the waiting was in progress in the past.

Regular verbs form the past tense by adding -*ed* to the verb. However, there are many irregular verb forms that you must learn. Here are two ways to learn these verb forms. In your journal, write down all the irregular verb forms you come across in your studying. Then, write your own sentences using the simple past form and the past participle form. Also, try to learn three or four new irregular verbs each day. Irregular verb forms are listed in Appendix D, pages 266–269.

ACTIVITY C-2-2   In the following paragraph, the verbs have been left out. Using the verb in parentheses, write the correct tense and form of the verb. The first one is done as an example.

1. I _was_ (be) really scared when I _got_ (get) my first traffic ticket.

2. Last Christmas, my friends and I _____ (drive) to Houston.

3. It _____ (be) my first time to take a trip in the United States and I _____ (be) really excited.

4. As we _____ (drive) out of New Orleans on I-10 west, there _____ (be) many cars on the highway.

5. When we _____ (pass) the airport, the traffic _____ (get) lighter, so we _____ (speed) up hoping to arrive at our destination before sunset.

6. We _____ (use) a radar detector so that we would know where the police were.

7. Just at that time, the car in front of me _____ (go) really slow, so I _____ (decide) to pass it.

8. As I _____ (speed) up, the radar detector _____ (start) to make a warning sound.

9. We _____ (be) scared because the police car _____ (be) just on the shoulder of the highway.

10. I _____ (be) afraid the police would follow us, but my friend just _____ (joke) and _____ (say), "Come on, come on, catch us!"

11. Then we _____ (hear) the police car siren and I _____ (see) the police car approaching rapidly.

12. The police car _____ (be) behind us and _____ (motion) us to stop on the shoulder.

13. At that time, I _____ (not know) what to do because I _____ (never got) a traffic ticket before.

14. All I _____ (think) about was how much I would have to pay for the ticket.

15. I _____ (get) out of the car and the policeman _____ (ask) me for all my documents.

16. He _____ (write) down all the information.

17. He also _____ (keep) my driver's license and _____ (give) me a temporary driver's license.

18. Finally, I _____ (get) back in the car and we _____ (continue) on to Houston. Such an awful thing to happen at the beginning of our vacation!

—Hsin-Chuan Chen

Simple Present Tense for Explaining

In a narrative, writers use past tenses to tell the story, but they may use **simple present tense** when they explain or comment about the story. Writers use the simple present tense to explain how they feel or think now about incidents that happened in the past.

ACTIVITY C-2-3   Read this paragraph and do the activities that follow.

I felt surprised, then happy, then doubtful all in one split second when I found out I had been chosen to be a star in the school play. That was my dream, to stand on the stage to give a performance. When the notice was published, everyone congratulated me. At that time, I felt happy about it; on the other hand, I felt nervous. I asked myself, could I give a good performance on the stage? Could I adapt to playing in front of a crowd? Could I speak loud enough in the play? When I thought about these problems, my jaw shook. But I decided I would try my best to be a good actor. I had been in the drama society for two years. I had learned some acting skill, but that was not enough for the play. The play would be opening in two months. I rushed into the frenzied business of rehearsal. Gradually I got used to it, and I even began to enjoy acting. The night of the performance came. No sooner had the curtain gone up than my eyes were confronted with thousands of gleaming eyes in the darkness. I stood on the stage and spoke, but my hands and legs were trembling. My voice didn't tremble, so I looked full of confidence, but, in fact, I was very nervous. When the curtain fell, the audience gave us a big hand and cheered. Then we knew we had done a good job in the play. When the curtain went up again, we gave thanks to the audience, but the cheer sounded louder than before. At that time I felt I had won an Oscar for the best actor. When we finished all of the work after the play, we took some pictures as a memento. Now, I keep a copy of that picture on my dresser. When I look at this picture, I think about the cheer from the audience, the events during rehearsal, and the personal satisfaction of entertaining the people. That memory will be in my mind forever.

—*Chi (Matthew) Wong*

1. Divide the paragraph into two parts: the part that tells the story and the part that comments on it. Draw a line between the two parts.
2. What tenses are used in the part of the paragraph that tells the story?
3. Find an example of a simple past tense, a past perfect tense, and a past continuous tense. Why are these tenses used?
4. What tenses are used in the sentences that comment on the story? Why?

ACTIVITY C-2-4   The following narrative paragraph has some errors with verb forms and tenses. Underline the verb/tense errors, write the correct verbs, and explain why you used the verb form or tense you did.

One day I was hired to work for a tree company. My first day of work with this company was the beginning of a new experience which was very dangerous. We were in a place out of town. We begin to work under high power lines cutting small trees. Robert, my partner, was cut them with a big machete and I was spraying them to kill the roots of the trees. We are about one hundred yards from the truck when we have heard a strange noise coming from the brush which was two or three feet away from us. We couldn't see anything. I jump away from there; at the same time, Robert hit his machete again and again until the noise stop. Then, he had put his hand in the brush and pulled out a big rattlesnake. That experience I had the first day of work was only the beginning of more exciting things that happen to me.

—Victor Amaya

Used To and Would

The expressions **used to** and **would** indicate actions that occurred on a regular basis in the past. They tell about actions that were habits or customs. In descriptive writing, the writer sometimes tells about an activity that occurred over and over in the past.

I **used to** study from Wednesday to Saturday.
We **would** ask each other to clear up the questions.

The writer often introduces the activity with *used to* and then continues with *would*.

I **used to** visit a park almost every weekend. There **would** usually be a crowd of people standing around the entrance. They **would** be talking and joking.

ACTIVITY C-2-5   Think about what you used to see on your way to school when you were a child. Make a list of what you saw. Get a partner and tell him or her what you used to see. Then write a short paragraph about it.

Adverbial Clauses of Time

Writers may use **adverbial clauses of time** to show the relationship of events. Adverbial clauses of time answer the question **when.** Adverbial clauses are dependent clauses with a subordinator.

The following subordinators introduce adverbial clauses of time:

ADVERBIAL CLAUSES OF TIME

SUBORDINATOR	EXAMPLE
while, when, as, whenever	**While** I was driving away, the driver copied my license plate number.
	When we got to school, I changed my mind.
before, after	**Before** we could think of what to do next, the teacher appeared in the door.

until	We were friends **until** I told the teacher about the vase.
as soon as, the moment that, once	**As soon as** I found out I wasn't convicted, I exhaled slowly.
	The moment that I saw her, I thought she was pretty.

ACTIVITY C-2-6   The following paragraph could be improved with adverbial clauses of time. Connect the pairs of italicized sentences below, using a subordinator from the chart above.

The school was very big, with a number of buildings and a large playground. I stood in front of the main hall of the school, watching the students pass by. The time passed quickly but I didn't realize it. Carrying my school bag, I wondered which direction I should go to get to my classroom. (1.) *The bell rang. All the students rushed into their classrooms.* I was the only one standing in front of the main hall. A prefect walked toward me and told me where my class was. (2.) *I walked into the class. Everyone stared at me as if I were a strange guy.* (3.) *The teacher asked me to take a seat. I felt I was doing something wrong.* After the first lesson, the class began to be noisy. All the students were busy talking to each other, but nobody talked to me. I was left alone sitting at the back in a corner near the window. (4.) *I looked out the window. I saw a lot of students playing soccer, which was my favorite game.* Suddenly the teacher shouted my name and I jumped up. Because I was not paying attention in class, I was punished by being made to stand on a chair. (5.) *The whole class laughed at me. I felt so embarrassed.* During recess, I followed the students to the food stores to buy some food to eat. Later, I had a stomachache, so I went to the lavatory. The school bell rang and the class was over. All the students rushed to go home. When I came out of the lavatory, nobody was in the classroom. (6.) *I stood in front of the school. The only thing I could hear was the sound of birds that came from some trees.* On the street, cars moved with a hustle and bustle. (7.) *The sky became darker and darker. The houses began switching on lights.* Slowly, I walked back home.

—*Cheng Kooi Koay*

ACTIVITY C-2-7   Read the pairs of sentences below and do the following.

1. In your notebook, combine the pairs of sentences into one sentence with one of the time subordinators from the chart above.

2. Write out your new sentence and add the appropriate punctuation.
3. Finish the story.

It Was a Dark and Stormy Night

1. I was home alone studying. Suddenly, the power went out.
2. I started to get up from my desk to look for a candle. I heard a long, loud knock at my bedroom window.
3. I heard the knock. My heart started to pound.
4. I stared at the window for an eternity. Then I . . . (finish the story)

ACTIVITY C-2-8   Think of a short folk tale from your culture. Make a list of the events in the tale. Write the story in a paragraph, using the appropriate tenses and adverbial clauses of time.

Appendix C-3: Grammar Review, Chapter 3

Verb Tenses

Past Tenses for Past Description

The verb tense used in descriptive writing depends upon whether the writer is describing a place he or she remembers from the past or a place that is part of his or her present life.

In writing about places from the past, the writer uses **past tenses.** You may want to review the past tenses in Appendix C-2, pages 221–227.

ACTIVITY C-3-1   Read the following paragraph from Renata Strakova's description, "Our Cottage." Underline the past tense verbs. Tell which past tense the writer uses.

> In the room were a wooden sofa with dark red cushions, a coffee table, and three armchairs. These things had been in our house before my parents brought them to the cottage. They were old and worn, but comfortable. There was a worn red carpet on the floor that was almost the same color as the sofa. In the corner was a small table with an old black and white TV. We didn't use it very often when we were at the cottage, but it was nice to have it there. It also had come from our house.

Simple Present Tense for Present Description

To write about places that are part of the writer's present life, he or she will use **simple present tense.**

> Probably the living room **is** my most favorite room of all because we often gather together after we **come** home from work or school.

SIMPLE PRESENT TENSE

Simple present tense is used to indicate:

general ideas and truths

> *Example*
>
> The walls of the living room **are** pink.

habitual action

Example

We **receive** our guests in the living room.

mental perceptions or emotions

Example

The living room **is** my favorite room.

ACTIVITY C-3-2   Read the paragraphs below and do the activities that follow.

I met Amy on the second day of my arrival in New Orleans. My friend took me to her apartment to introduce me. Amy and I got along right away, so I decided to move in with her because she was looking for a roommate. Our apartment is pretty and comfortable, but especially it is very homey.

My apartment has a living room, kitchen, bathroom, and one bedroom. I like the living room very much because Amy and I spend most of our time there. The walls are a warm pink color. On the wall, there are some big pictures of sailboats, which Amy loves. There are a couch, TV, and a small table beside the window, which has curtains with pretty pink and blue flowers to match the walls. Also the room contains a light green corduroy chair, many CDs, some magazines, and a lot of pictures of Amy and my friends on the door. The carpet is moss green. Everything is not new; in fact, it all seems used a lot, which makes the room very homey.

—*Chiemi Hashio*

1. Underline the simple present tense verbs.

2. Find simple present tense verbs that indicate the following and write them below.

   a. General idea or truth: _____

   _____

   b. Habitual action:_____

   _____

   c. Mental perception:_____

   _____

3. Some verbs are in the past tense. Circle any past tense verbs you find. Why are these verbs in the past tense?

ACTIVITY C-3-3   On a separate sheet of paper, draw a sketch of a room on campus, for example, the classroom you are in, the cafeteria, the entrance to the library. Get a partner and take turns describing the room each of you has sketched.

Sentence Structures for Location

There + Be

A useful sentence structure for stating location is *there + be*. Look at these examples.

> **There is** a sofa next to the piano.
> **There are** light colored curtains on the window.
> **There was** a tall forest of dark green spruce trees.
> **There were** cliffs that rose for hundreds of feet.

In this sentence structure, the word *there* is not the subject. The subject follows the form of the verb **be** (*is, are, was, were*). The verb must agree with the subject that follows it.

SENTENCE STRUCTURE: *THERE + BE*

	VERB	SUBJECT	COMPLEMENT
There	was	a worn red carpet	on the floor.
There	are	some pictures	on the wall.

This sentence pattern is often used to introduce a description. The sentence that follows it is usually a different sentence pattern and gives detail about the item introduced.

There are some pictures on the wall. One of the pictures is a photograph of my mother.

ACTIVITY C-3-4   Look at the photograph on the next page and do the following.

1. Choose three items in the photograph to describe.

2. For each item, write two sentences using the present tense. Use *There is/There are* in the first sentence. In the second sentence, give more detail about the item.

The first one is done as an example.

1.a. There is a coffee table in front of the fireplace.

  b. It is small and square.

2.a. _____

  b. _____

3.a. _____

  b. _____

4.a. _____

  b. _____

Adverb/Verb/Subject

Another useful sentence structure for stating location is adverb of place/verb/subject.

SENTENCE STRUCTURE: ADVERB/VERB/SUBJECT

ADVERB OF PLACE	VERB	SUBJECT
On the right side	were	wheat fields.
In the corner	was	a small table.
In the opposite corner	stands	a Sony television.
On the wall	is	a picture of the sea.

In this sentence structure, the adverb of place begins the sentence. The subject follows the verb but must agree with it.

This sentence structure is useful in writing description because it shows spatial relationships. It gives cohesion between two sentences, especially if the noun in the adverb of place has been mentioned in the previous sentence.

I could see for miles down the **valley. In the valley** were some ponds.

She greeted us when we walked in the **door. To the left of the door** was the fireplace.

ACTIVITY C-3-5   Find a picture of a place in a magazine or draw a sketch of a place. With a partner, tell where items are located.

Subject-Verb Agreement

Look at the following verb forms. What difference do you notice between those in Column One and those in Column Two?

SUBJECT-VERB AGREEMENT

	ONE			TWO	
I	like	this room.	He	likes	this room.
You	like	this room.	She	likes	this room.
We	like	this room.	It	likes	this room.
They	like	this room.			

The verbs in the second column have an -s on them while those in the first column do not. The verbs in the second column have subjects that are third-person singular. When the subject is third-person singular, the verb that goes with it has an -s. This feature is called **subject-verb agreement.** This just means that if the subject is the pronouns *he, she, it,* or a word or phrase for which you can substitute *he, she,* or *it,* the verb must have an -s on it.

SUBJECT-VERB AGREEMENT

ONE	TWO
They like this room.	She **likes** this room.
The students (= they) like this room.	My mother (= she) **likes** this room.
The teachers in this building (= they) like this room.	My cat (= it) **likes** this room.
	The man in room 305 (= he) **likes** this room.

Subject-verb agreement can be difficult in sentences with the following features:

1. The subject is separated from the verb by other words.
    The **paint** on the walls **is** a soft blue.

2. The sentence has two subjects.
    The **couch** and the **chair are** light green corduroy.

3. The subject looks plural but takes a singular verb. *News, politics, the United States, economics, athletics, series,* and *electronics* take singular verbs.
    The **news** on television **is** depressing.

4. The subject is a word, or is modified by a word, expressing the idea of quantity. *Each, every, everybody, everyone, someone, somebody, either, one, no one, nobody,* and *neither* take singular verbs. *All, some, a lot of, no,* and *none* take either singular or plural verbs depending on whether they are used with countable or uncountable nouns.
    Each of the chairs **needs** to be fixed.
    One of the windows **has** a gold curtain.
    Some of the tables **are** old-fashioned.
    Some of the furniture **is** new.

5. The sentence has verbs in a sequence that agree with the subject. All the verbs must have the -s, not just the first one.
    He **looks** out the window, **thinks** about his family, and suddenly **feels** lonely.

6. The sentence begins with *There is/There are*.
   There **is a picture** on the wall.
   There **are windows** on two sides of the room.

7. The sentence structure is adverb of place/verb/subject.
   On the right side **were** wheat **fields**.
   On the walls **is** a **picture** of my family.

8. The subject is a gerund or infinitive.*
   Painting houses **is** hard work.
   To find a new apartment **takes** time.

ACTIVITY C-3-6   In the following sentences, circle the subject and give the correct form of the verb.

1. Our English classroom _____ (have/has) several unusual features.

2. One strange thing about it _____ (are/is) its shape.

3. It _____ (are/is) a long, narrow room, only about six feet across.

4. This _____ (mean/means) that there _____ (are/is) space for only about three chairs in each row.

5. Another unusual feature of this room _____ (are/is) that it _____ (have/has) no windows.

6. There _____ (are/is) only blank walls on all four sides.

7. To me, this aspect of the room _____ (are/is) depressing.

8. Our teacher often _____ (bring/brings) a picture of a window to put on the wall.

9. The picture _____ (show/shows) a beautiful field with the sun shining on it.

10. When she _____ (put/puts) the picture on the wall, it _____ (brighten/brightens) up the room.

ACTIVITY C-3-7   Read the paragraphs below and find the subject-verb agreement errors. First find the main subject and verb of each sentence. Change the verb if it does not agree with the subject. Some sentences do not have errors.

1. I never get tired of the view from my balcony. I live in an apartment building that overlook the Pacific Ocean. In this part of California, the coastline is a bit rugged. About two hundred feet out, there

Look at Appendix C-5, pages 243–250, if you want to study gerunds and infinitives.

is big red and grey rocks jutting up out of the ocean. So when I look out, I see huge waves crashing against the rocks, sending spray up into the air. The waves roar and foam and then falls back into the ocean. I often sit out on my balcony in the afternoons and just look at the waves. Even though the beach are rugged, there are always a lot of activity on the beach. A lot of people walks up and down the beach and just sit on the rocks. There is one man who comes every day at the same time. He wear old tennis shoes and carry a bucket. He walks out on the rocks and search in the tide pools for the small creatures that lives in them. I always wonder what he find. There is also a woman who I imagine is a photographer. She often come to the beach at sunset bringing her camera equipment. She gets into all kinds of strange poses trying to get the perfect sunset picture. As for me, I just sit on my balcony and watch life as it unfold before me.

2. One of my favorite places is the Majestic Theater in my home town. It is the only theater in town, so everybody meet there on Saturday nights to go to the movie. It always bustle with activity. My friends and I gather outside the theater under the bright flashing lights of the marquee, which announce the movie. As we line up in front of the tiny ticket booth to the left of the big glass double doors, we joke and laugh and push each other, sometimes getting a bit rowdy. When it is almost time for the movie to start, my friend Peter remind us that it is time to move into the lobby, which smell of people and hot buttery popcorn, and get in line at the snack counter. As soon as we pay for our extra-large bags of popcorn and extra-large Cokes, we head through one of the side doors on each side of the snack counter and into the theater. For a moment, our eyes sting with the darkness, but we know our way so well that we move quickly down the aisle, past rows of talking people, to the very front row. Just as the music begin, we settle in to watch whatever movie is showing.

Appendix C-4: Grammar Review, Chapter 4

Verb Tenses

Present Perfect Tense

When the writer is analyzing or explaining, he or she will often use the **present perfect tense** (*has* or *have* + **past participle**). The present perfect is used to refer to an event in the past, but the past time of the event is not the important focus. The important focus is the effect that the past action or event has on the present time and on the writer. The present perfect always ties the past to the present.

I **have** always **admired** my first-grade teacher, Mr. Pauls.
She **has reflected** a bright image to every pupil who has crossed her path.

PRESENT PERFECT TENSE

Present perfect tense is used to indicate:

events that occurred at some unspecified time in the past (often with already, just, or yet)

> *Example*
>
> He **has** already **decided** to major in business administration.

events that occurred more than once in the past

> *Example*
>
> He **has changed** his major three times.

events that began in the past and continue to the present (often with *since* or *for*)

> *Example*
>
> I **have changed** a lot since I came to this school.

ACTIVITY C-4-1   How have you changed since you came to this school? Write five sentences below telling how you have changed.

1. _____

2. _____

3. _____

4. _____

5. _____

ACTIVITY C-4-2 Read the following paragraph and fill in the appropriate form of the verb. Use either the simple present, simple past, or present perfect tense.

For most people, there has been a moment in their lives when they have changed their attitude. Recently, I _____ (become) a father and I _____ (experience) a change in my attitude toward my parents. Before becoming a father, I _____ (be) the son of my parents. My parents _____ (take) care of me and I _____ (not think) too much about my parents' love because I thought it was the usual thing. After I became a father, I _____ (realize) how difficult it _____ (be) to take care of a baby, so I _____ (come) to admire my parents and their generation. In my parents' generation, there _____ (be) no gas stoves, microwaves, dishwashers, dryers, and other electric appliances to help women do the housework. Women _____ (have) to wash clothes by hand and spend a lot of time cooking and cleaning. Also, in my country it _____ (be) taboo for the man to help the woman with the housework and with taking care of the baby. But nowadays, this custom _____ (change). In my case, I _____ (help) my wife do the housework and take care of the baby. The conditions under which my parents' generation _____ (take) care of children _____ (be) worse than now, but they _____ (do) well. So, I _____ (come) to admire my parents and their generation.

—*Inho Hong*

Consistency of Verb Tenses

Usually a writer is consistent with verb tenses. A piece of writing usually has one main tense. The writer may switch to another tense, but only for a particular reason. If there is no reason or need to switch, the tense of the piece of writing will be consistent. When the writer switches tenses, he or she often signals this switch with a time word.

ACTIVITY C-4-3 Read the following sections of Kristin Hunter's essay and answer the questions.

The teacher who did the most to encourage me was, as it happens, my aunt.

She was Myrtle C. Manigault, the wife of my mother's brother Bill, when she taught me in second grade at all-black Sumner School in Camden, New Jersey. Now she is Mrs. Myrtle M. Stratton, retired and residing in Haddonfield, New Jersey.

1. Underline all of the main verbs in these paragraphs.
2. What is the main tense the writer uses? Why?
3. What tense does the writer switch to? Why does she switch? What time words signal the switch?

During my childhood and youth, Aunt Myrtle encouraged me to develop every aspect of my potential, without regard for what was considered practical or possible for black females. I liked to sing; she listened to my voice and pronounced it good. I couldn't dance; she taught me the basic jitterbug steps. She took me to the theater—not just children's theater but adult comedies and dramas—and her faith that I could appreciate adult plays was not disappointed.

Aunt Myrtle also took down books from her extensive library and shared them with me. We had books at home, but they were all serious classics. Even as a child I had a strong bent towards humor, and I will never forget the joy of discovering Don Marquis's *Archy & Mehitabel* through her.

Most important, perhaps, Aunt Myrtle provided my first opportunity to write for publication. A writer herself for one of the black newspapers, the Philadelphia edition of the Pittsburgh *Courier*, she suggested my name to the editor as a "youth columnist." My column, begun at age fourteen, was supposed to cover teenage social activities—and it did—but it also gave me the latitude to write on many other subjects as well as the habit of gathering material, the discipline of meeting deadlines, and, after college graduation six years later, a solid portfolio of published material that carried my byline and was my passport to a series of writing jobs.

4. What is the main tense used in these paragraphs? Why? What is the time signal at the beginning of the third paragraph?
5. The writer switches tense once. What tense does she switch to? Why?

Today Aunt Myrtle, independently and through her organization (she is a founding member of The Links, Inc.), is still an ardent booster of culture and of her "favorite niece." She reads omnivorously, attends writers' readings, persuades her clubs to support artists, and never lets me succumb to discouragement for very long. As I told her theater club recently, she is "as brilliant and beautiful and tough as a diamond." And, like a diamond, she has reflected a bright, multifaceted image of possibilities to every pupil who has crossed her path.

6. What is the main tense of this paragraph? Why? What is the time signal at the beginning of the paragraph?
7. There is one past tense verb. Find it. Why is it used?
8. What tense is used in the last sentence? Why? Is there a time signal for this tense? Why or why not?

CONSISTENCY OF VERB TENSES

VERB TENSE	TIME FOCUS
The teacher was my aunt.	past truth
Now she is Mrs. Myrtle M. Stratton.	present truth
She provided my first opportunity to write.	past action
I will never forget the joy of discovering a new book.	future truth
She has reflected a bright image to every pupil who has crossed her path.	present effect of past action

Hunter consistently uses one main tense, but she shifts to other tenses when she needs them. She signals the tense shifts with time words so her readers will not be confused.

ACTIVITY C-4-4   In the following paragraph, underline the main verbs. Identify the verb tenses and be ready to tell why each verb tense is used.

One reason people lie is to achieve personal power. Achieving personal power is helpful for someone who pretends to be more confident than he really is. For example, one of my friends threw a party at his house last month. He asked me to come to his party and bring a date. However, I didn't have a girlfriend. One of my other friends, who had a date to go to the party with, asked me about my date. I didn't want to be embarrassed, so I claimed that I had a lot of work to do. I said I could easily find a date even better than his if I wanted to. I also told him that his date was ugly. I achieved power to help me feel confident; however, I embarrassed my friend and his date. Although this lie helped me at the time, since then it has made me look down on myself.

—*Mo Fung (Jackie) Chan*

ACTIVITY C-4-5   The following paragraph has some errors in verb tenses. Find the errors, fix them, and be ready to explain what was wrong.

It was hard to choose a suitable school when I had applied to some American universities last year. I didn't understand anything about America before I come here. Because I have never been to the United States at that time, all the information about schools came from the news, magazines, some institutes, and my friends. I get I-20 forms from about eight schools, but I finally decide to come to this one. There were several reasons I chose the University of New Orleans. The first reason was financial. Because of my limited resources, I have to choose a school that is fairly inexpensive. That meant I couldn't choose a private school or even most states' public universities. This school was not too expensive so it fitted my requirement. The second factor was the location of the school. Because I am used to living in a big city, I couldn't bear the life of a small town. I would rather see crowds and buildings instead of cattle and grassland. Although New Orleans isn't a really big city like New York, there are about one million people living in the metropolitan area. Additionally, New Orleans is famous for its tourism, which was very attractive to me.

—*Hsin-Chuan Chen*

Adjective Clauses

In writing description or analysis, a writer must give detail. One way to present detail is to use **adjective clauses.** Adjective clauses are dependent clauses that describe or modify a noun. They follow nouns and are introduced by **relative pronouns.**

ADJECTIVE CLAUSES

PRONOUN

who, that, whom (for people)

which, that (for things)

whose (for possession)

Examples

She has reflected a bright image to every pupil **who** has crossed her path.

She has reflected a bright image to every pupil **that** has crossed her path.

The people **whom** I spoke to also admired her.

The people (   ) I spoke to also admired her.

I had a solid portfolio of published material **which** carried my byline.

I had a solid portfolio of published material **that** carried my byline.

The portfolio **that** I developed in that job was my passport to a series of writing jobs.

The portfolio (   ) I developed in that job was my passport to a series of writing jobs.

The pupils **whose** lives she touched will never be the same.

ACTIVITY C-4-6   The following paragraphs could be improved with adjective clauses. Combine the pairs of italicized sentences below. Make one of the sentences into an adjective clause that modifies a noun in the other sentence.

Examples: People have all kinds of dreams. These dreams brighten up their lives.
People have all kinds of dreams that/which brighten up their lives.

Most people have dreams. I know these people.
Most people that/whom I know have dreams.

Sports utility vehicles, or SUVs, like the Jeep Cherokee, Ford Explorer, and Nissan Pathfinder were originally intended for use in wild, rugged places like deserts and mountains, places where ordinary cars couldn't go. (1.) *Yet you see thousands of them in American cities and suburbs being driven by middle-class people. These people will never see a desert or mountain in their lives.* Why has this kind of car become so popular with people who live in the city? In my opinion, Americans buy cars to fulfill their dreams and people buy SUVs because they dream of adventure.

Most Americans have a dream car. (2.) *It is the car. This car suggests to them what they would like to be.* For some people, it's a sophisticated Ferrari; for others it's a comfortable family van; for others it may be a big, showy Cadillac. (3.) *When I was a teenager, the car was the Ford Mustang. I dreamed about this car.* I thought the Ford Mustang was extremely cool. It was sporty, with plenty of power under the hood. (4.) *It indicated a sophisticated lifestyle. I craved this lifestyle.* I imagined myself driving around town in this wonderful car, knowing everyone was admiring me. Of course, I never had a Ford Mustang; it was only a dream.

(5.) *In the same way, I think people have a dream of going on wonderful adventures around the world. These people buy SUVs.*

They would like to climb Mount Everest, cross the Sahara Desert, and explore Tierra del Fuego. Of course, most of them never will. (6.) *They have jobs. These jobs keep them in the city.* They are accountants, engineers, teachers, secretaries, and plumbers. (7.) *Also, many of them have children. These children have to go to school, soccer games, and the shopping mall.* With jobs and families, these people will usually drive no farther than downtown to work or to a park on the weekends. (8.) *However, that doesn't mean they can't dream of going to places. These places sound exotic.* And so they buy a Jeep Cherokee, with four-wheel drive and heavy-duty suspension. In their dreams they are getting ready to head to Timbuktu.

ACTIVITY C-4-7   Complete each sentence with an adjective clause.

1. I am a person _____

    _____

2. For me, a dream car is one _____

    _____

3. People _____

    _____

4. The kind of car _____

    _____

5. A dream _____

    _____

Appendix C-5: Grammar Review, Chapter 5

Passive Voice

In writing about a process, a writer may use passive voice. Look at these examples:

OPAC **is used** by many students.
The system **has** recently **been installed.**

Passive voice focuses attention on the action (verb) or the receiver of the action (object) in a sentence instead of on the doer (subject) of the sentence.

PASSIVE VOICE

Active voice verb:

Someone **connects** these parts together.

Passive voice verb:

These parts **are connected** together by someone.

To change an active sentence to a passive sentence:

1. begin the sentence with the object of the sentence
2. add a form of *be* or *get* and change the main verb to the past participle
3. add *by* before the subject

Active voice: The company **bought** a computer.

Passive voice: A computer **was bought** by the company.

Often the *by* phrase is left out.

Passive voice: The computer **is used** every day.

Here is a simple test to see if you have a passive sentence. Can you add *by someone* to the verb? Does it make sense? If so, the verb is passive.

The computer *was used* **by someone.**
The machine *is being installed* **by someone.**
The printer *could be returned* **by someone.**

ACTIVITY C-5-1   Underline the complete verb phrase in the following sentences. Decide if the verb phrase is active or passive. (Use the *by someone* test.)

1. The university has installed a new computer system.
2. The new system can be used by both faculty and students.

3. The computer terminals are located on the first floor in the computer science building.
4. To use a computer terminal, students must present their IDs.
5. Then they are given a personal code number which gives them access to the system.
6. The same process is used by faculty members.

Use the passive voice in these situations:

1. when the doer is not important
2. when the doer is unknown
3. when you want to avoid identifying the doer
4. when you want to focus on the action or receiver of the action

ACTIVITY C-5-2   Read the following paragraph and do the following activities.

Students now have access to more materials in the university library because the library has been computerized. A new system called OPAC (Online Public Access Catalog) has been installed. Through this system, all of the university libraries in the state are linked together. This means that the holdings in all the libraries in the state are available to students. The OPAC computer terminals are located on the first floor of the library. They can be used whenever the library is open. Instructions for using the OPAC system are given on printed guides next to the computer and on the computer screen. The staff at the Information Desk can also offer help.

1. Underline the passive voice verbs.
2. Change the passive voice verbs to active voice.
3. Think about how the new verbs change the paragraph.

Which version of the paragraph is better? Why?

The passive voice is often used in academic writing in science and technology to give the writing objectivity. The focus in science is on the object or result of the research, not the person doing the research. Thus, the scientist will write "the process was completed" rather than "I completed the process."

ACTIVITY C-5-3   Read the following paragraphs about the camera obscura, taken from an encyclopedia. Decide if the verb should be passive or active and fill in the correct form.

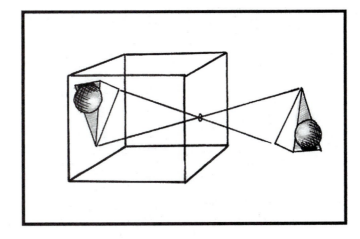

The simplest form of the camera obscura _____ (consist) of a box that is lightproof except for a small hole in one side. Light from external objects _____ (enter) the hole and _____ (form) an inverted image on the opposite side.

The term *camera obscura* _____ (be) Latin for "dark chamber." The inventor and date of invention _____ (not know). The device, however, _____ (use) before A.D. 1000 to observe eclipses and to aid in sketching from nature.

If the image side of the box _____ (make) of translucent paper or ground glass, the image _____ (can view) from outside the camera. If the image side _____ (be) opaque, the chamber must be considerably larger so that viewing _____ (can do) from inside the camera. Some types of the camera obscura _____ (have) a lens, a prism, and a mirror.

Gerunds and Infinitives

In writing about a process, a writer often finds gerunds and infinitives useful. Gerunds (**verb** + **ing**) and infinitives (**to** + **verb**) are verb forms used as nouns. Like nouns, they can be used as subjects and objects in a sentence.

Look at these sentences:

Learning this skill takes patience.
You need **to insert** the diskette.

What is the subject of the first sentence? What is the verb? What is the verb of the second sentence? The object?

In the first sentence, the subject is *learning* and the verb is *takes*. In the second sentence, the infinitive *to insert* is the object of the verb *need*.

Here are some guidelines for using gerunds and infinitives:

1. Gerunds (not infinitives) are usually used as subjects of sentences. A gerund subject is singular.

   Using a videotape machine **is** not complicated.

   ACTIVITY C-5-4   Finish these sentences.

   1. Using a computer _____

   2. Going to the library _____

   3. Understanding how ____ works _____

   4. Planning a party _____

   5. Getting married _____

   6. Having children _____

   7. Moving to another city _____

2. Gerunds are used as objects of some particular verbs.

   I enjoy **making** movies with my video camera.

VERBS FOLLOWED BY A GERUND

admit	get around to	regret
advise	get out of	relate
appreciate	imagine	remember
avoid	include	report
can't help	keep on	resent
confess	mention	resist
consider	mind	resume
debate	miss	risk
delay	picture	save
deny	postpone	stop
discuss	put off	succeed in
dislike	protest	suggest
enjoy	practice	take up
escape	quit	welcome
feel like	recall	work at
finish	recommend	understand

ACTIVITY C-5-5   Complete the following sentences using a gerund.

1. Can you imagine not _____

2. You shouldn't avoid _____

3. I appreciate _____

4. Don't delay _____

5. My roommate dislikes _____

6. I feel like _____

7. Do you resent _____

8. Don't even consider _____

9. You can't get out of _____

3. Gerunds are used as objects of prepositions.

He is good at **operating** the equipment.

(The gerund *operating* is the object of the preposition *at.*)

VERB + PREPOSITION FOLLOWED BY A GERUND

admit to	cry about	look forward to
agree on	decide against/on	object to
allude to	depend on	pay for
approve of	dream about	plan on
argue about/against	end with	refer to
ask about	fight about	speak about/of
balk at	figure on	start with
begin with	forget about	talk about
believe in	hear about	tell about
care about	inquire about	think about/of
center on	insist on	warn about/against/of
confess to	laugh about	wonder about
count on	lie about	worry about

ACTIVITY C-5-6 Choose ten of the verbs above and write sentences about yourself. Use a gerund after the verb/preposition.

Example: I have never worried about falling asleep at night.

4. Infinitives can be used as subjects, but this use is quite formal. It is more common to begin with the dummy subject *It* followed by an infinitive.

To get a driver's license is easy.   (formal usage)
It is easy **to get** a driver's license.   (more common usage)

ACTIVITY C-5-7 Change each sentence to one that begins with *It* and includes an infinitive. The first one is done as an example.

1. Buying all of the components for my new computer was expensive.

   It was expensive to buy all of the components for my new computer.

2. Getting all of the parts out of the boxes wasn't too difficult.

   _____

   _____

3. Learning how to hook up all the parts of my computer was a challenge.

   _____

   _____

4. Understanding the computer manual was really hard.

   _____

   _____

5. Becoming familiar with the word-processing program required patience.

   _____

   _____

6. Getting help from a friend was a good idea.

   _____

   _____

5. Infinitives are used as objects of some particular verbs.

   He decided **to get a** driver's license.

VERBS FOLLOWED BY AN INFINITIVE

agree	fail	promise
appear	get	refuse
arrange	guarantee	request
ask	happen	seem
attempt	have	tend
beg	hope	threaten
care	intend	try
choose	learn	used
decide	manage	want
desire	mean	wish
endeavor	need	
expect	plan	

ACTIVITY C-5-8   Choose ten verbs from the chart above and write ten sentences telling what you have done in the last several days. (Use the present perfect tense.)

Example: I have agreed to go out with my friends on Saturday night to celebrate my friend's birthday.

6. Infinitives without *to* are used as objects of some particular verbs such as *let, make, help,* and *have.*

He let me **use** his video camera.

(The verb *let* is followed by the bare infinitive form *use* as the object of the sentence.)

ACTIVITY C-5-9   Read the introductory sentences below and do the following:

1. Underline the gerunds and infinitives.
2. Make a list of five sentences that suggest how a person can make friends at a new school. Use gerunds and infinitives in your sentences if appropriate.

Going to a new school can be a scary experience. You don't know where anything is and you don't have any friends. The best way to get accustomed to finding your way around is first to take a tour of the school. This will help you learn where the buildings are. Then, you will want to make some new friends. Making new friends is easy if you follow these steps.

1. *You can begin by speaking to someone in class.* _____

2. _____

3. _____

4. _____

5. _____

6. _____

Appendix C-6: Grammar Review, Chapter 6

Comparative Forms

To write comparison and contrast, a writer will use a number of comparative structures. Read the sentences below and underline the comparative forms.

TOEFL requirements at University A are lower than at University B.

The dormitories are more comfortable at University B than at University A.

Paying tuition goes faster at University B than at University A.

Registration moves more quickly at University A than at University B.

University A has more students than University B.

University B has more area than University A.

Study the chart below.

COMPARATIVES OF INEQUALITY

	ONE SYLLABLE	TWO SYLLABLES	
Adjective	lower	more comfortable	than
Adverb	faster	more quickly	than
Plural Count Nouns	more students		than
	fewer students		than
Noncount Nouns	more area		than
	less area		than

Read the sentences below and underline the comparative forms.

The students at University B are as smart as those at University A.

The English Language Program at University A runs as smoothly as the program at University B.

The jazz band at University A is the same size as the one at University B.

Study the chart below.

COMPARATIVES OF EQUALITY

Adjective	as	smart	as
Adverb	as	quickly	as
Noun	the same	size	as

Read the sentences below and underline the comparative forms.

In my opinion, University A is better than University B.

The dormitory food is worse at University B than at University A.

Study the chart below.

IRREGULAR COMPARATIVE FORMS

Adjective	good	better
	bad	worse
Adverb	well	better
	badly	worse

ACTIVITY C-6-1   With a partner, study the following graph. Discuss the questions and write your answers.

Foreign Students[1] Enrolled in Institutions of Higher Education in the United States, 1985–1986 and 1995–1996[2]

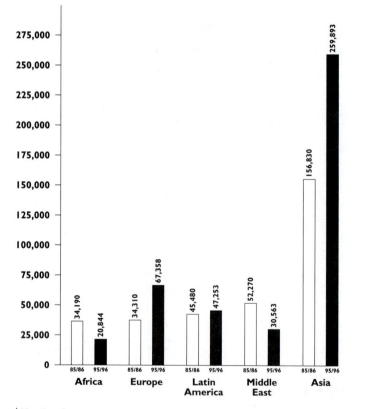

[1] Non-Immigrants

[2] Source: *Digest of Education Statistics,* 1999, Published by the National Center for Education Statistics, Office of Educational Research and Development, U.S. Department of Education.

1. What is being compared in this graph?
2. What do the numbers at the left of the graph represent?
3. What conclusions can you draw from this graph? (Draw at least six conclusions.)

ACTIVITY C-6-2   With a partner or by yourself, study the following graph and write answers to the questions.

Average Annual Income by Education and Sex–1998[1]

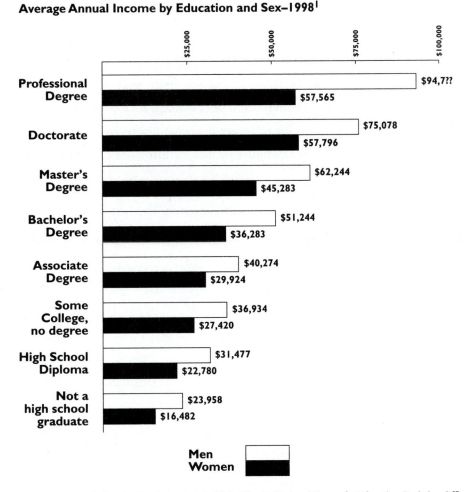

[1] Source: *Digest of Education Statistics,* 1999, Published by the National Center for Education Statistics, Office of Educational Research and Development, U.S. Department of Education.

1. What is being compared in this graph?
2. What is the main conclusion or generalization you make from this graph?
3. Write at least six sentences to support this generalization.

Correlative Conjunctions

To write comparison and contrast, a writer may use correlative conjunctions. Correlative conjunctions are pairs of words or phrases that work together. Look at these pairs of words.

both . . . and
not only . . . but also
either . . . or
neither . . . nor

Each pair connects structures that have the same grammatical form. You can use nouns, adjectives, verbs, gerunds, infinitives, and so on. Read the sentences below and circle the correlative conjunctions. Underline the structures they connect and label them.

Both Mr. Thomas and Mr. Smith teach chemistry.

Mr. Thomas is not only young but also talented.

Mr. Smith either reads from his notes or writes on the chalkboard.

Mr. Smith enjoys neither lecturing nor grading papers.

ACTIVITY C-6-3 Combine the pairs of sentences below into one sentence with the correlative conjunctions given. The first one is done as an example.

1. (both . . . and) All majors must take a course in history. All majors must take a course in biology.

   All majors must take both a course in history and a course in biology.

   _____

2. (not only . . . but also) Courses in business are interesting. Courses in business are useful.

   _____

   _____

3. (either . . . or) Engineering majors usually take four years to finish their degree. Engineering majors may take five years to finish their degree.

   _____

   _____

4. (neither . . . nor) The teacher did not enjoy the class. The students did not enjoy the class.

   _____

   _____

5. (both . . . and) Liberal Arts majors must take a course in mathematics. They must take a course in the physical sciences.

_____

_____

6. (either . . . or) We can not classify English as a physical science. We can not classify English as a biological science.

_____

_____

Run-on Sentences

There are two common mistakes in punctuation. One is a run-on sentence. In this case, two sentences (independent clauses) are written as one, with no punctuation between them. (If you do not understand clauses, review Appendix C-1.)

Read the following run-on sentence. Underline the two sentences and circle the place where there should be some punctuation.

My calculus teacher seemed to be tired every day he was not enthusiastic about helping students to solve their math problems.

You can correct a run-on sentence in four ways. Study the chart below.

CORRECTING RUN-ON SENTENCES

1. Make two complete sentences. Put a period between the two clauses.

   . . . day. He . . .

2. Make one complete sentence. There are three ways to do this.

   a. Put a semicolon between the two clauses.

      . . . day; he . . .

   b. Connect the two clauses with a coordinator.

      . . . day, so he . . .

   c. Connect the two clauses with a subordinator.

      Because my calculus teacher was tired every day, he was not enthusiastic about helping students to solve their math problems.

Comma Splices

The other common punctuation error is putting only a comma between two independent clauses. This error is called a **comma splice**. A comma by itself cannot connect two independent clauses. Read the sentences below and circle the comma that is a comma splice.

He often brought many notes and books to class, during the class period, he seemed to look at the lesson for the first time.

You can correct a comma splice in the same ways as you correct a run-on sentence.

CORRECTING COMMA SPLICES

1. Make two complete sentences. Put a period between the two clauses.

   . . . **class. During** . . .

2. Make one complete sentence. There are three ways to do this.

   a. Put a semicolon between the two clauses.

      . . . **class; during** . . .

   b. Connect the two clauses with a coordinator.

      . . . **class, but during** . . .

   c. Connect the two clauses with a subordinator.

      Even though he brought many books and notes to class, during the class period, he seemed to look at the lesson for the first time.

You are likely to make a comma splice when you use sentence connectors. Circle the comma splice in the sentence below.

He thought that education was not so important in people's lives, therefore, he suggested that the weaker students should find other ways to survive in their lives.

To correct this sentence, put a period or a semicolon before *therefore*.

. . . **lives. Therefore,**
. . . **lives; therefore,**

Which of the above ways you choose to correct a run-on sentence or a comma splice depends upon your meaning. In general, if the two clauses are not closely related in meaning, make two sentences; if the two clauses are closely related in meaning or if combining them can show the relationship of ideas more clearly, make one sentence.

ACTIVITY C-6-4   Identify and correct the run-on sentences and comma splices in the following sentences. Write the correct sentences on a separate sheet of paper.

1. The buildings are larger at Osmania University than at Kakatiya University, also, Osmania has more buildings than Kakatiya.

2. Osmania has a large space for sports and games, Kakatiya has only a small space for sports.

3. Osmania has a large library with many books Kakatiya has a smaller library with fewer books.

4. The cafeteria at Osmania University is bigger and cleaner than the one at Kakatiya it also has some video games.

5. At Osmania University, attendance is really necessary, if a student misses one class, he is going to miss a lot.

6. The teachers give a lot of homework, also, they give exams on alternate weeks.

7. After a couple of weeks, the teachers check the progress of the students on the homework and exams, if they are unsatisfied with some students, they move them to a lower level class.

8. At Kakatiya University, students do not have any tests up to the final exams, therefore, the students do not concentrate on their studies until the last minute.

—Purnachander Thangada

ACTIVITY C-6-5   Read the following paragraphs and correct any errors in run-on sentences and comma splices.

The admission requirements of universities in the U.S. are easy. Students who have completed high school can enroll or continue their study in the university, normally, the university will only require students' high school academic record. On the other hand, the admission to Malaysia University is more restricted only those students who have passed their high school exam with flying colors can enroll in the University. In other words, the number of students who qualify to go to university in the United States is very large, while the number who qualify in Malaysia is small.

The American education system is more flexible than Malaysia's education system. In the United States, students can choose any subject that they want to study, for example, an electrical engineering student can choose the subjects without exactly following the course schedule stated by the University. He may choose psychology first instead of taking mathematics. Unlike the course schedule in the United States, the course schedule in Malaysia University is fixed students studying in any major field have to follow the course schedule exactly. If they do not follow the course schedule, they may be suspended from studying for one semester. The other difference is that students in the United States can choose whether they want to study in the summer Malaysian students have to complete their courses without an intermediate break.

—*Koay Cheng Kooi*

Appendix C-7: Grammar Review, Chapter 7

Parallel Structure

In writing classification, the writer uses parallel structure. Parallel structure means using the same grammatical form for two items or for items in a series. You can use clauses, phrases, adjectives, nouns, or adverbs. Look at the different structures below.

PARALLEL STRUCTURE

Examples

Adjectives Consumer magazines are popular and easily available.

Infinitives The purpose of these magazines is to inform and to entertain.

A series of nouns *Consumer Reports* gives consumers information on car prices, models, and mileage.

ACTIVITY C-7-1   In each sentence, underline the parallel structure and identify its form. The first one is done as an example.

1. Consumers usually read these magazines <u>quickly</u> and <u>easily</u>. *adverbs*
2. Consumer magazines make money because they have the most readers and because they carry the most advertising.
3. They are sold at newsstands and by subscription.
4. News magazines tell about events that happen locally, nationally, and internationally.
5. *Time* magazine reported on the death and destruction caused by the Kobe earthquake.
6. These magazines also report on national news, popular culture, and current lifestyles.
7. Because they are current, entertaining, and interesting, many people rely on them for the news.

ACTIVITY C-7-2   In the following sentences, underline the item in the series that is not parallel and correct it.

1. Trade publications are suitable for those people who have businesses or to learn more about their business.
2. They give many ideas on how to expand their business or making money.
3. *Heavy Duty Trucking* appeals to truckers and those who want to buy a truck.

4. It is an appealing and interest magazine for a specialized audience.

5. *American Medical News* is read by doctors, people doing research, and scientists.

6. Professional magazines are expensive and you can only find them in certain places.

ACTIVITY C-7-3   Complete the following sentences with parallel items.

1. Consumer magazines can be divided into two kinds: those appealing to men and _____.

2. Men's magazines often include articles on ways to keep fit like body building, _____, and _____.

3. They also have feature stories on popular and _____ men like Shaquille O'Neal, _____, or _____.

4. They may have articles about investing or _____ money.

5. The advertising is designed to make men buy _____ and _____.

6. Women's magazines usually center around clothes and _____.

7. Sometimes there are articles about how to organize your day, _____, and _____.

8. They may have articles about getting along with the boss or _____.

9. They often include advice on love and _____.

10. The advertising in women's magazines usually focuses on _____, _____, and _____.

Sentence Fragments

A fragment is a piece of something broken off from a larger whole, like a fragment of paper torn off from a sheet of paper. Similarly a **sentence fragment** is a piece of a sentence that has been punctuated as a complete sentence. It is part of a sentence that needs to be made into a complete sentence. Following are the most common causes of fragments:

1. A fragment is a dependent clause or phrase.

    CNN is a TV station that always provides us with world news. **Which is very useful for foreigners.**
    Seeing the Kobe earthquake on CNN. He was so worried about his family.

Both the clause (*Which is very useful for foreigners*) and phrase (*Seeing the Kobe earthquake on CNN*) above are dependent structures that cannot be sentences by themselves. Dependent clauses and phrases must be attached to independent clauses. Thus, the way to correct these fragments is to attach them to independent clauses to make a complete sentence.

CNN is a TV station that always provides us with world news, **which** is very useful for foreigners.

Seeing the Kobe earthquake on CNN, **he** was so worried about his family.

2. A fragment can be missing a subject.

Is a good station to watch because it announces a lot of necessary news.

To correct the fragment, add a subject to make a sentence.

It is a good station to watch because it announces a lot of necessary news.

3. A fragment can be missing a main verb.

"Eye Witness News" one of the most popular TV shows to watch in the morning.

To correct the fragment, add a verb to make a sentence.

"Eye Witness News" **is** one of the most popular TV shows to watch in the morning.

ACTIVITY C-7-4   Find the fragments in the following sentences and correct them.

1. We can divide the news into two kinds. Hard news and soft news.

2. Hard news consists of important events at the local, national, or international level. Like the new state sales tax, the presidential election, or the war in Afghanistan.

3. Usually, hard news is reported by the most famous reporters. Those who have big names like Peter Jennings or Tom Brokaw.

4. When reporters tell about hard news. They are serious and try to be objective.

5. Soft news, on the other hand, not considered so important.

6. Soft news, for example, the reactions of citizens to a new movie or a report on the president's wife's visit to a nursery school.

7. The people who report the soft news usually people you have never heard of. They are new or unknown reporters.

8. The reporting style of people reporting soft news. Is more friendly and less serious than the style of those reporting hard news.

9. Is interesting to note the differences between these two types of news.

10. Sometimes, I prefer the soft news. Because it is more cheerful.

ACTIVITY C-7-5   Find and correct any sentence fragments in the following para-graph.

American novels can be divided into two groups according to quality. The first group consists of books we call classics. These books have depth and insight about human nature. Have stood the test of time. People continue to read them even if they were written a long time ago. These books are studied in high school and college litera-ture classes. So that young American will have some knowledge of the highest quality American writing. Some examples of American classics *The Scarlet Letter* by Nathaniel Hawthorne, *Huckleberry Finn* by Mark Twain, and *The Age of Innocence* by Edith Wharton. In reading these books. We see in the characters the problems and difficulty we all face in life. The second group of American novels consists of popular books. Which are popular for a short period of time and then fade away. Often, they are superficial in their understanding of human character or they are not very well written. In any case, they do not stand the test of time to become classics. Examples of popular books. The suspense novels of Stephen King and the murder mysteries of Sue Grafton. These books are entertaining but don't give us insight about ourselves.

Appendix C-8: Grammar Review, Chapter 8

Adverbial Clauses of Result

To tell results, a writer can use **adverbial clauses of result.** This structure combines two clauses: the first clause tells a quality or characteristic about the topic and the second clause tells the result. Look at this example.

The microwave oven is so easy to use that children can use it.

What quality about microwave ovens is being discussed?

They are so **easy** to use.

What is the result of their being easy to use?

That **children can use them**.

Read the sentences below. Circle the quality named in the first clause and underline the result clause.

It works so quickly that many fast food restaurants use it.
It has so many attractive features that everyone wants one.
It is such a popular appliance that some families have more than one.

Adverbial clauses of result are introduced with the subordinator *so/such . . . that*.

Study the chart below.

ADVERBIAL CLAUSES OF RESULT

SO...THAT	
adjective	so easy that
adverb	so quickly that
much, many	so many attractive features that
few, little	so few people that
SUCH...THAT	
noun	such a popular appliance that

ACTIVITY C-8-1   In the following sentences, circle the quality being discussed. Then complete the sentence with the result that makes sense.

1. Telephone answering machines are so popular that _____

_____

2. Answering machines come in so many different styles that _____

_____

3. Some people think they are such a nuisance that_____

_____

4. Other people think they are so convenient that _____

_____

ACTIVITY C-8-2   Below are listed some common technological inventions and innovations. With a partner or by yourself, do the following.

1. Choose six of the inventions. For each one, brainstorm a list of its qualities. Be as specific as you can.
2. Then write down the results of those qualities.
3. Finally, write a sentence using *so/such . . . that.*

Example

Weather satellites

accurate	can predict hurricanes days in advance
expensive	not all television stations can buy them
have many capabilities	are used for many purposes

Weather satellites are so accurate that they can predict hurricanes days in advance.

computers
fax machines
VCRs
beepers
cellular telephones
photocopying machines
freeways
digital cameras
radar
scanners in grocery store checkouts
subways
heart bypass surgery

Reduced Adverbial Clauses

Adverbial clauses of time and reason with active verbs (or with the auxiliaries *be* or *have)* can be reduced to a phrase with *-ing.* To reduce these clauses, the adverbial (dependent) clause must have the same subject as the independent clause.

> After I waited at a bus stop for about twenty minutes, I got on another bus to go back home.

> After waiting at a bus stop for about twenty minutes, I got on another bus to go back home.

> Because he needed to go to the store, he had to take a bus.

> Needing to go to the store, he had to take a bus.

ACTIVITY C-8-3   If possible, reduce the sentences below by making one of the clauses a phrase. If the sentence cannot be reduced, write "Not Possible."

1. While he was waiting for the bus, he glanced at his watch.

   _____

   _____

2. When the bus came, it was full.

   _____

   _____

3. Because he was frustrated, he sat down angrily on the bench.

   _____

   _____

4. Because I did not have a lot of money, I used to go to school by bus.

   _____

   _____

5. When I got on the bus, I remembered leaving my English book at home.

   _____

   _____

6. When the bus stopped, I got off.

   _____

   _____

7. After I went back home and got my book, I got back on the bus.

   _____

   _____

8. Because I did not have a car, I wasted both time and money.

   _____

   _____

APPENDIX D: Irregular Verb Forms

SIMPLE FORM	PAST FORM	PAST PARTICIPLE
be	was, were	been
bear	bore	born
beat	beat	beat
become	became	become
begin	began	begun
bend	bent	bent
bet	bet	bet
bind	bound	bound
bite	bit	bitten
bleed	bled	bled
blow	blew	blown
break	broke	broken
breed	bred	bred
bring	brought	brought
build	built	built
burst	burst	burst
buy	bought	bought
catch	caught	caught
choose	chose	chosen
come	came	come
cost	cost	cost
creep	crept	crept
cut	cut	cut
do	did	done
dig	dug	dug
draw	drew	drawn
drink	drank	drunk
drive	drove	driven
eat	ate	eaten
fall	fell	fallen

SIMPLE FORM	PAST FORM	PAST PARTICIPLE
feed	fed	fed
feel	felt	felt
fight	fought	fought
find	found	found
fit	fit	fit
flee	fled	fled
fly	flew	flown
forbid	forbade	forbidden
forget	forgot	forgotten
forgive	forgave	forgiven
freeze	froze	frozen
get	got	gotten
give	gave	given
go	went	gone
grind	ground	ground
grow	grew	grown
hang	hung	hung
have	had	had
hear	heard	heard
hide	hid	hidden
hit	hit	hit
hold	held	held
hurt	hurt	hurt
keep	kept	kept
know	knew	known
lay	laid	laid
lead	led	led
leave	left	left
lend	lent	lent
let	let	let
light	lit	lit
lie	lay	lain

SIMPLE FORM	PAST FORM	PAST PARTICIPLE
lose	lost	lost
make	made	made
mean	meant	meant
meet	met	met
pay	paid	paid
put	put	put
quit	quit	quit
read	read	read
ride	rode	ridden
ring	rang	rung
rise	rose	risen
run	ran	run
say	said	said
see	saw	seen
seek	sought	sought
sell	sold	sold
send	sent	sent
set	set	set
shake	shook	shaken
shine	shone	shone
shoot	shot	shot
shut	shut	shut
sing	sang	sung
sink	sank	sunk
sit	sat	sat
sleep	slept	slept
slide	slid	slid
speak	spoke	spoken
speed	sped	sped
spend	spent	spent
spin	spun	spun

SIMPLE FORM	PAST FORM	PAST PARTICIPLE
split	split	split
spread	spread	spread
spring	sprang	sprung
stand	stood	stood
steal	stole	stolen
stick	stuck	stuck
strike	struck	struck
swear	swore	sworn
swim	swam	swum
take	took	taken
teach	taught	taught
tear	tore	torn
tell	told	told
think	thought	thought
throw	threw	thrown
understand	understood	understood
wake up	woke up	woken up
wear	wore	worn
weave	wove	woven
weep	wept	wept
win	won	won
wind	wound	wound
wring	wrung	wrung
write	wrote	written

GLOSSARY

This glossary gives brief definitions of some of the difficult words from the readings in each chapter. The number after the definition is the page number on which the word is introduced.

About-face   reversal, change   174
Access   entrance, admission   99
Accumulation   gathering, collection   174
Acoustic array   pattern of sounds   199
Affiliation   connection, association   167
Anticipate   predicts, forsee   147
Antique shops   stores that sell very old and valuable items   16
Ardent   strong, enthusiastic   74
Artifacts   very old objects once used by humans   199
Awkwardness   uncomfortable feeling   47

Bad debts   unpaid bills   175
Bass   a kind of fish   147
Block   building   68
Booster   supporter   74
Byline   writer's name on a story   74

Cab   the part of a truck where people sit   48
Canopy   top part, roof   48
Cater to   try to please   147
Cockpit   place where airplane pilot sits   48
Colonel   high level officer in the military   49
Collided with   hit, struck   31
Condemned   considered bad   174
Contemplated   thought about   94
Confident of   sure about the quality of   5
Confirm   prove that something is true   115
Confucius   Chinese philosopher and teacher   68
Conservative   cautious, careful   175
Criticisms   negative comments   175
Culprit   guilty person   31
Cut the engine   turn off the engine   48

Daze   dream, confusion   47
Delegation   group   168
Densities   numbers of items in a given area   115

Détente   a decrease in tensions between two countries   121
Discipline   training in self-control   5
Dispatched   sent out   197
Distinguished   known, famous   121
Distract   take one's thoughts away from something   69
Done a complete about-face   changed completely, been reversed   174
Dotted around   located here and there   69
Drone   monotonous, steady sound   48

Eaves   edges of a roof   68
Egotism   selfishness   32
Elusive   hard to find   115
Enhanced   added to   68
Entrepreneur   person who starts and manages a business   147
Ethics   standards of right and wrong   122
Excavation   digging to find buried objects   199
Expedition   journey of discovery   115
Extensive   very large   68

Grappling   struggling, fighting   94
Grasshopper   a kind of drink   43
Ground-penetrating   passing through the ground   199

Harmonious   balanced, pleasing   54
Hefty   large   176
Heirlooms   items passed from generation to generation   54
Helmet   protective head covering   48
Hispanic   Spanish-speaking   48
Hosts of   a lot of   5

Image (verb)   make a picture of   199
In a daze   confused; dreaming   47
Incense   something that is burned to give a pleasant smell   68
Inclinations   interests, likings   121
Initial   beginning   5
Initiates   begins, causes to happen   197
Inner reaches   hard-to-find places   115
Intricate   complicated, heavily decorated   54

Jitterbug   a type of dance   74

Latitude   freedom   74

Lawn   area covered with grass   55
Literate   able to read and write   139

Mandatory   necessary, required   121
Minute (adj.)   very small   5
Miscellaneous   several different   31
Morals   standards of right and wrong   121

Noninvasive   not requiring that objects be cut or broken into   199
Nourishing   healthy   180

Objective   fair, impartial   168
Orchard   group of fruit trees   6

Panorama   a wide view   54
Penetrating   going through   199
Penmanship   learning to form the letters of the alphabet   5
Phony   false, dishonest   175
Pin down   identify exactly   95
Portfolio   collection (of work)   74
Potential   possible abilities   74
Prejudicial to   against, not in favor of   167
Prevalent   common   94

Radical   extreme, perhaps violent, person   175
Relic   object from the past   175
Resolution   the clarity of a picture   199
Rummage through   search in a disorganized way   175

Sentimental   emotional, nostalgic   54
Sergeant   low-level officer in the military   49
Shrill   high-pitched, loud   48
Sophisticated   cultured, aware of the world   47
Sprinters   racers who run in short, very fast races   107
Spruce   a kind of evergreen tree   54
Stockholders   people who own part of a company   148
String of bad debts   series of unpaid bills   175
Stunned   too upset to speak   31
Subscribers   people who receive a magazine regularly at home   147
Subsidiary   company controlled by another company   175
Suffer injustices   receive unfair treatment   139
Suicide   killing oneself   94

Tarnish its public image   make itself look bad   168
Taxi (verb)   drive an airplane on the ground   48
Terrace   an area beside a house with tables and chairs   54
Treadle   foot-powered   54
Tricky   difficult, confusing   95

Urge   strong desire   5

Warm up   prepare the body for physical activity   106

INDEX

Photo Credits

Page 1: Frank Siteman Studios
Page 3 top and bottom: Frank Siteman Studios
Page 4 top: Michael J. Doolittle/The Image Works
Page 4 bottom: Ralf-Finn Hestoft/Index Stock Imagery
Page 28: Julie Dennis/Index Stock Imagery
Page 49: Associated Press/TASS/Wide World Photos
Page 51: Kindra Clineff/Index Stock Imagery
Page 70: Frank Pedrick/The Image Works
Page 72 left: Rick Friedman
Page 72 right: AFP/Andres Ballesteros/Corbis
Page 73 left and right: Reuters/Corbis-Bettmann
Page 93: Eastcott-Momatiuk/The Image Works
Page 94: David Lassman/The Image Works
Page 97: Ellen Senisi/The Image Works
Page 100: Bob Daemmrich/The Image Works
Page 107: Bob Daemmrich/The Image Works
Page 117: Larry Kolvoord/The Image Works
Page 120: Frank Siteman Studios
Page 147: Hazel Dunlop/Eyecatchers/The Image Works
Page 143: Frank Siteman Studios
Page 170: Zefa Visual Media-Germany/Index Stock Imagery
Page 172 top: Michael Keller/Index Stock Imagery
Page 172 bottom: Frank Siteman Studios
Page 173 top left: Bill Lai/Index Stock Imagery
Page 173 bottom left: Frank Siteman
Page 173 top and bottom right: Frank Siteman Studios
Page 173 middle right: Larry Lawfer/Index Stock Imagery
Page 196 top: Chip Henderson/Index Stock Imagery
Page 196 bottom: Stewart Cohen/Index Stock Imagery
Page 198 top: John Eastcott/The Image Works
Page 198 bottom: David Kohl/AP/Wide World Photos
Page 233: Zephr Picture/Index Stock Imagery

Text Credits